THE ASPIRING SCREENWRITER'S DIRTY LOWDOWN GUIDE TO FAME AND FORTUNE

THE **ASPIRING SCREENWRITER'S**
DIRTY LOWDOWN GUIDE
TO FAME AND
FORTUNE

Tough Lessons You Need to Know
to Take Your Script from
Premise to Premiere

ANDY ROSE

🦌 ST. MARTIN'S GRIFFIN 🦌 NEW YORK

THE ASPIRING SCREENWRITER'S DIRTY LOWDOWN GUIDE TO FAME AND
FORTUNE. Copyright © 2018 by Andy Rose. All rights reserved. Printed in
the United States of America. For information, address St. Martin's Press,
175 Fifth Avenue, New York, N.Y. 10010.

www.stmartins.com

Designed by Steven Seighman

The Library of Congress Cataloging-in-Publication Data is available upon
request.

ISBN 978-1-250-15949-6 (trade paperback)
ISBN 978-1-250-15950-2 (ebook)

Our books may be purchased in bulk for promotional, educational, or
business use. Please contact your local bookseller or the Macmillan Corporate and Premium Sales Department at 1-800-221-7945, extension 5442,
or by email at MacmillanSpecialMarkets@macmillan.com.

First Edition: February 2018

10 9 8 7 6 5 4 3 2 1

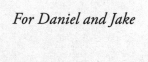

For Daniel and Jake

CONTENTS

ACKNOWLEDGMENTS

Many thanks to the following:

My boyhood influences, including *Mad* magazine, Neil Simon, *Laugh-In*, George Carlin, *SNL*, Woody Allen, and *National Lampoon*, all who inspired me to be creative and funny, and showed me you don't need to have a real job to make a living.

My family, especially my mother, who trusted me and was supportive when I told her I was moving to LA to pursue screenwriting after she just spent a fortune on my college education and assumed I would become a doctor.

My agent, Jeff Silberman, who believed that a new book on movie-writing could sell in a crowded marketplace and worked with me on fifty-seven drafts of a proposal (at least it seemed like that many), and to my editor, Michael Homler, for believing in it as well.

The numerous Hollywood producers and executives whom I've worked with over the years, some talented motivators, others now in the vinyl siding business.

The Ohio State University Film Studies Department for giving me the opportunity to teach what I know, and to all my students, even the ones who complain about having to get to class at the ungodly hour of 9:35 in the morning, two days a week. Wait till you have kids!

SO YOU WANT TO BE A SCREENWRITER

True story.

Upon completing my very first screenplay at the ripe old age of twenty-three, a bubbly character actress living in the Los Angeles apartment building next to mine offered to show it to a few people she knew "in the business."

"Sure!" I said, excitedly. After all, my only other Hollywood connection back then was my great-aunt Fannie, who had recently married a retired real estate mogul named Manny (yes, their actual names), whose sister was Bob Hope's longtime secretary. I figured that Bob, who was pushing ninety at the time, was probably not interested in a rowdy youth comedy, so I chose not to pursue that somewhat tenuous contact.

Anyway, about a week after giving this bubbly character actress a stack of freshly bound scripts, she left me an urgent phone message. Seemed an established movie director was "jazzed" about my screenplay and I needed to meet him that afternoon at a certain address on Sunset Boulevard.

Ecstatic, I slid into my Sergio Valente designer jeans, grabbed my Members Only jacket, and raced off as visions of drinks with Spielberg, Lucas, or Coppola danced in my head. We would discuss how great my script was, line up a few more projects, and then talk about whether I should buy my first house in Beverly Hills or Malibu.

As it turned out, the director was not the renowned auteur behind *Jaws, Star Wars,* or *The Godfather.* His claim to fame was *The Happy Hooker Goes to Washington,* and drinks ended up being a warm can of Coke on the roof of his aging West Hollywood apartment. He did, however, express interest in directing my script. All I had to do was raise the money.

I know, depressing, right? But this book was not written to tell you how easy it is to make it as a screenwriter in Hollywood. It was written to tell you how tough it is to even try. Those of you brazen enough to ignore this warning and pursue your creative dream anyway should be prepared for years of rejection, frustration, and disappointment. There are twelve thousand members of the Writers Guild of America, five hundred thousand other wannabe writers, and six hundred movies released every year. Do the math, my aspiring scribes.

Okay, before you shred this book and send me hate mail, let me tell you the good news. You can beat the odds. That's right. YOU. CAN. BEAT. THE. ODDS. I did, and so did dozens of other people I know from small towns and big cities across America. Some had Ph.D.s, others were high school dropouts. Most started out knowing little about movies other than to avoid the bubble gum stuck under the seats at the local multiplex. But in order to make it as a screenwriter, you have to have knowledge. That is what this book is about. It provides you with all the basics you need to know from both a creative and business perspective. If you know how to navigate the waters, you have as good a chance as anyone else to fulfill your dream.

I've been a professional Hollywood screenwriter for more than twenty-five years, as well as a screenwriting instructor at Ohio State University for the past nine. During my time as an educator, I have read many books on scriptwriting and am always eager to recommend new literary wisdom to the zealous minds that I teach. After all, any book that extols the virtues of proper structure, natural dialogue, three-dimensional characters, and compelling subplots has value. Exactly how much? That's the big question.

Far too many of the books I've read are written in long-winded, analytical chapters, picking apart the various elements of screenwriting like a vulture dissecting a dead cow. While these authors' analyses of the subject matter may be ingenious, deciphering what they say and putting it to practical use is seldom an easy task for the fledgling writer.

In addition, very few of these books spend much time talking about the business side of screenwriting from a raw and candid perspective. How do you break in? Can you really make a living at it? What kinds of deals do writers get? How do you get representation? Simply obtaining a list of literary agents from the Writers Guild—which many of these books recommend—is about as useful as tossing your script over the surrounding moat of a movie star's home and thinking he or she is actually going to read it.

Unsatisfied with the books offered on the market, I was faced with a dilemma when I first started teaching at the college level. I needed to come up with written material to use as my classroom text, but none of the books that I found seemed suitable for the course I wanted to teach. My students had little experience in writing movies, and the last thing I wanted to do was scare them off with a thick, intricate text that made them feel like they were in over their heads. (My blunt ramblings about the struggles of the young writer would scare them off enough, thank you.)

That's when I decided to create my own set of handouts. They would be specific, to the point, easy to comprehend, and provide a good basis to introduce a writer to moviewriting. And as you should realize by now, I don't hold any punches.

This book is a compilation of all my handouts, along with my own personal experiences (or war stories) that I recount weekly to my class. Hopefully, by reading this book, you will not make the same mistakes I made when I first got started, such as turning down an offer from Disney to write *The Little Mermaid* ($211 million worldwide gross) because I didn't want to waste my time on some dumb kiddie cartoon.

My analysis of the many aspects of screenwriting is

simple but powerful. Everything is presented in a workbook-like fashion to help the reader start, and finish, a feature film screenplay and get it out into the marketplace. I go over all facets, step by step, from developing a simple premise to turning it into a potential sale. This book can be used as a classroom text, or simply by the wannabe writer who doesn't have access to (or the finances for) more sophisticated instruction.

So start working on your ideas. Then start writing. It all begins with Fade In.

PART ONE

THE CREATIVE SIDE
OF SCREENWRITING

NAME YOUR GENRE

What's your favorite type of movie? The one where the brawny hero leaps into his sleek sports car and races the heinous villain down a treacherous mountain road? Or perhaps it's an old-fashioned Dodge City standoff between two gun-slinging cowboys battling over stolen gold? Or maybe you prefer a lighthearted chick flick where the clumsy boy pursues the dreamy girl, and captures her heart in the end? Clearly, all of these movies are distinctly different, and that's because they belong to different genres.

Genre is the artistic category of a film defined by its style, content, and form.

Consider a story about a jewel heist. It could be a thriller, or an action/adventure film, or even a broad comedy. It all depends on the writer's approach to the subject matter. You need to figure out in which genre (or genres) you would like to write, and this is usually determined by the kinds of movies you like to see. There are numerous genres recognized in the world of cinema. The main ones are as follows:

1) **DRAMA:** True to life stories of a serious nature. They are realistic and rely on genuine character relationships and intense emotional involvement. Some may be biographical (*Lincoln*), political (*All the President's Men*), or historical (*Schindler's List*) in their premise. But all should touch the hearts of the viewers, and even bring out the hankies to dry their eyes. Other examples of dramas include *Nebraska, The King's Speech, Cool Hand Luke, The Shawshank Redemption.*

2) **SCIENCE FICTION/FANTASY:** These movies are usually set in a future timeframe (*Star Trek*) or in an imaginary world (*Harry Potter and the Sorcerer's Stone*). The characters often include nonhumans, and the writer establishes the rules of what they can and cannot do. All rules, no matter how unreal in our contemporary world ("Beam me aboard, Scotty!") must be presented in a credible manner. These films are a total escape from reality, but that's exactly why we go to the movies—real life is boring. Other examples include *The Matrix, Alien, The Princess Bride, The Wizard of Oz.*

3) **COMEDY:** Stories in this category approach a subject using humor. The audience better be laughing, or at least chuckling, when watching your movie. Otherwise,

your comedy becomes a tragedy. Since there are many types of comedy, we can divide them into subgenres:

a) **Romantic Comedy:** Love stories that put a smile on your face. (*Pretty Woman, The Wedding Singer, Annie Hall, The 40-Year-Old Virgin, Sleepless in Seattle*)

b) **Black Comedy:** Serious matter dealt with in a comedic way. (*The War of the Roses, Eating Raoul, Dr. Strangelove or: How I Learned to Stop Worrying and Love the Bomb, Harold and Maude, Throw Momma from the Train*)

c) **Teen Comedy:** Appeals to teenagers and involves school, dating, pimples, proms, and the issues that affect today's youth. (*American Pie, Fast Times at Ridgemont High, Superbad, Clueless, Mean Girls*)

d) **Broad Comedy:** Very unrealistic and revolves around slapstick jokes and physical humor more than character development or believable plots. (*Airplane!, The Hangover, Animal House, Blazing Saddles, Monty Python and the Holy Grail*)

e) **Action Comedy:** A serious story, often crime-related, but with lots of physical humor and dialogue played for laughs. (*Beverly Hills Cop, 21 Jump Street, Rush Hour, Ghostbusters*)

4) **ACTION ADVENTURE:** These stories present characters who tackle dangerous events with lots of physical action. There may be brief moments of humor, but the char-

acters are on a serious mission with dire consequences. Examples include *Die Hard, Raiders of the Lost Ark, The Dark Knight, Mission: Impossible, Goldfinger.*

5) **THRILLER:** Suspense and mystery abounds in these films. The audience should be on the edge of their seats as they follow the protagonist's journey. Examples here include *Chinatown, Se7en, North by Northwest, The Silence of the Lambs, The Fugitive.*

6) **FAMILY:** Stories that are suited for kids and, if done well, also tolerable for their parents. They may be live action (*Beethoven*), animated (*Toy Story*), or a musical (*Mary Poppins*). Other examples include *Frozen, E.T., Babe, Finding Nemo.*

7) **HORROR:** These movies usually contain graphic content, meant to scare viewers out of their seats. The good ones have clever stories and work from a psychological perspective (*The Exorcist*). Today, however, we often equate horror movies with slasher films (*Nightmare on Elm Street*). Other examples include *Rosemary's Baby, Night of the Living Dead, Friday the 13th, Halloween, The Evil Dead.*

8) **WESTERN:** Films in this category deal with the emerging frontier. Think cowboys, horses, saloons, and lots of gunfire. Examples are *Unforgiven, High Noon, The Treasure of the Sierra Madre, The Wild Bunch, True Grit.*

9) **DOCUMENTARY:** These are unscripted stories about real people and events. But just because there's no script,

it doesn't mean the movie is void of structure. A narrative needs to be laid out and the dots need to be connected. However, the bulk of the writing is done in the editing room and not on the page. Examples include *Roger & Me, The Last Waltz, Amy, Woodstock, Hoop Dreams*.

Some writers work strictly in comedy, others science fiction. Some writers have no preference and can write any genre. Naturally, the more versatile you are, the better chances you have to get hired for a writing assignment. The main thing is to be comfortable writing in whatever genre you choose to tackle.

One thing to be aware of—many films fit into more than a single genre. For instance, *Star Wars* may be science fiction, but it is also an action adventure movie. *Little Miss Sunshine* is a drama, but it is also a comedy (or dramedy as it's commonly called). Being able to combine genres is a positive thing. It increases the potential audience for your movie, which means a bigger box office for the company producing it. In a business driven by revenue, this may make the difference in getting your film made.

Don't, however, try to force a crossover genre into your story simply in hopes of attracting a financier or a larger audience. Years ago, I wrote a very witty feature comedy for Universal Studios based on the '60s TV show *McHale's Navy*. Unfortunately, the producers decided it should also be an action adventure movie, so they had the script rewritten, sacrificing a lot of the humor for some physical, and expensive, set pieces. Despite my protests, I was just the writer—one notch below craft services on the feature film totem pole. There was nothing I could do about it except bang my head on the wall and cry. The end result was a film with neither enough laughs nor enough action to be successful in either genre, and the wrath of the critics, along with the empty seats in the theaters, let the producers know just that.

Think about the movies you like and identify what genre they belong to. If they all fit into the same category, that's clearly your favorite genre and probably the one in which you should be writing.

HERE'S AN IDEA

You know that old saying, "Ideas are a dime a dozen"? Well, not in the movie business. A good idea in Hollywood can be worth over a million dollars to a writer if it becomes a successful motion picture, once script fees, production bonuses, and residuals are tallied. I still get checks every few months for a film I wrote two decades ago, thanks to DVD sales in places like Mozambique and Kazakhstan. Finally, after all these years, I have found my true fan base!

But how do you come up with an ingenious idea? Certainly not by staring at a blank computer monitor and hoping that a brilliant concept magically leaps off the screen and invades your ravenous mind with dazzling inspiration (though wouldn't *that* be a great premise for a movie?). No, in order to find that amazing idea, your brain needs to be stimulated. And stimulation comes from the world around you.

Walk the dog, surf the internet, hit the mall, go to the gym, take a day trip. While doing so, be cognizant of your surroundings and think about whether the things bombarding your senses could somehow translate into a movie. This will require some creativity on your part. After all, movies often suspend reality, and it's highly unlikely that on any typical day you're going to come across green-skinned Martians, or witness a grisly murder, or find a million dollars that falls off a truck.

However, if you use your imagination, even life's mundane moments can lead to all sorts of possibilities. What if those coneheaded trick-or-treaters you saw walking down the street in costume really were green-skinned Martians who happened to land here on Earth on Halloween night and nobody realized it? Movie! What if that big lumpy bag of trash you saw the local minister toss into the dumpster actually contained the body of a parishioner who discovered that the pastor was embezzling church funds? Movie! What if those Boy Scouts selling popcorn on the street corner near where the armored truck is making a pick-up found a bag of cash left outside the vehicle and went nuts with the money? Movie!

Over the years, I've sold several pitches based on seemingly insignificant events that, with the proper embellishment, turned into wonderful movie ideas. Sometimes you actually see the incident, other times you read about it, or maybe it's based on something someone told you. This was the case with my first studio project, called *Modern Girls*. A college friend casually mentioned that two girls from her dorm had dressed up as guys to see if they could fool everyone and pledge a fraternity. They were quickly discovered and sent back to sorority row. No, not much of a movie there. But it got me thinking.

What if this became a story about two sweet girls who trash a snooty sorority house on rush night after the rude and uppity sisters ridicule their less-than-attractive friend to tears? The two girls are caught, and as punishment, get suspended from the college for a semester and kicked out of their dorm. Afraid to tell their parents, too broke to afford an apartment, and unable to be seen on campus, they decide to dress as guys and pledge a fraternity. They are accepted and move into the house. There they must deal with secretly being girls in a house of boys and adjust to male rituals, frustrated romances, and a suspicious frat brother. This idea sold to Universal Studios in five minutes.

Another idea came from something I saw. While waiting in line to retrieve my car from the parking valets at a posh LA bistro, I found the contrast of these poor teenage drivers riding off in hundred-thousand-dollar Porsches, Ferraris, and Mercedes to be quite intriguing (sadly, my vehicle was the old Mustang). How tempting it must be for them to take these expensive speed machines for a quick joyride while their hungry owners unwittingly dine inside the restaurant. Out of this, *Cruise Control* was born. It was a story about an annual race where one valet from each local restaurant had to take the valeted car of a guest and race it around town to various checkpoints before the owner's meal was done or they got discovered. The winner was crowned Car Jock for the year. This idea sold to Warner Bros.

And finally, sometimes ideas come out of something you read. I was perusing a magazine once and saw an ad for the Christian Children's Fund which featured actress Sally Struthers (*All in the Family*), who at the time was still a household name. In bold print, she stated that a donation of just eighteen dollars a month would feed a poor, malnourished African orphan for thirty days. Heart-wrenching photos of these adorable, sad-eyed toddlers beckoned for your contribution. It got me thinking. What if someone wanted to go beyond the eighteen dollars a month and actually adopt one of these children?

I conjured up a story in which a liberal, upper-class, middle-aged American couple, unable to have kids and unsuccessful in adopting one, decide to bring one of these needy orphans over to America and adopt him as their own. They pick out a small cute boy from pictures, make the necessary legal arrangements, and anxiously wait for his arrival. They figure the neighbors will be so impressed with how progressive they are, that they'll be the toast of the town. Turns out, the photos they saw were a bit dated. The boy they chose is now sixteen years old, 6'3", 220 pounds, and excited to be in his new home with all the modern amenities. As for the shocked couple, they must now examine their own values, prejudices, and responsibilities as parents while dealing with the lad's acclimation to America. I pitched this story, called *Big Bundle of Joy,* all over town. People loved it, and though this one never sold, it got me lots of meetings and helped me make some worthwhile contacts leading to future business.

When you're first starting out, the best ideas are ones we call "high concept." This means you can state the premise in a line or two and anyone can immediately see the possibilities of why this could be a great movie. There's nothing wrong with writing a script about the internal struggles of a lonely priest holed up in a dank monastery during the Spanish Inquisition, but you're best saving that story for after you win your first Academy Award. Be careful, however, that a high concept idea doesn't become a one-note movie where you keep repeating the same beat over and over. In *Click,* the premise of a man (Adam Sandler) being able to stop or fast-forward through time using a magical TV remote control is clever, but it becomes overdone and feels episodic, relying more on gimmick than on substance. But in the movie *Groundhog Day,* where a man (Bill Murray) must live the same day over and over, the story is much more skillfully constructed. Here, the beats change and progress unpredictably as the main character goes through some honest revelations.

Another way to generate ideas is to put a new twist on an existing idea. *Austin Powers: International Man of Mystery* was simply James Bond played for laughs. *Scream* took all the traditional conventions of slasher movies and satirized them. And anything in the public domain is fair game for an updating, often many times. Think of all the films based on *Romeo and Juliet.* There was *Valley Girl, Shakespeare in Love,* the all-time classic *West Side Story,* and lots more.

Producers also sell their own ideas to a studio, and then hire a writer to tackle the script. Usually, these ideas are nothing more than a basic premise for a film without any detailed story development. Competing writers will each take this concept, work out an entire story, and pitch it to the producer. He will choose the writer whose take he likes best. In order to beat out the other writers vying for the same job, you will need to come up with something fresh and unique. Think out of the box, but stay in orbit.

If you're lucky, however, in certain instances a producer may be such a big fan of your work, you're his first and only choice as the writer. This was the case when a producer with a studio deal pitched me a movie idea called *Kid Mayor.* It was about a teen who gets elected mayor of his small hometown and battles a bunch of old cronies for civic changes. Frankly, I thought it was one of the dumbest ideas I'd ever heard, but the president of the studio loved it and told me it was a done deal. All I had to do was work out a complete story with the producer and they'd hire me to write it. "Done deal, did he say?" Hmm, maybe this wasn't such a dumb idea after all. After a month of intense meetings, the producer and I came up with a pretty clever tale and I was actually happy I took the time to develop it. And as promised, the studio president immediately approved it and announced the new project to all his development execs at their weekly meeting. Unfortunately, *his* boss, the CEO of the studio, who rarely sat in on creative meetings, happened to sit in on that one. He thought it was one of the dumbest ideas he'd ever heard, and that was the end of *Kid Mayor.*

THE MIGHTY LOGLINE

Years ago, while I was shopping around a newly completed screenplay, a successful movie producer asked me to tell him what it was about. Unprepared, I quickly attempted to organize my thoughts and blurted out, "Okay . . . there are these boys . . . at a school . . . it's by an army base . . . and there's this instructor . . . he's really a spy . . . and uh . . ."

Hmm. Remember that famous line from the film *Jerry Maguire*, "You had me at hello"? Well I lost this producer at "Okay . . ." A writer needs to be able to describe his story confidently in a quick but expressive manner. The way to do this is with a powerful logline.

A logline is a one- or two-sentence description of your movie. It's similar to what a *TV Guide* blurb would be when describing a film. Though it may take all of five seconds to say or read, considerable time should go into its construction. Why? Because the logline is your first, and perhaps only, sales tool to get key members of the entertainment industry to read your script. Understand the facts:

A) Most screenplays written by inexperienced writers stink.

B) It takes well over an hour to read a feature length script.

C) No agent or producer wants to waste an hour of their life reading a stinky script.

No matter how good your screenplay may be, without a personal referral, you are just another one of the thousands of wannabe writers contacting people cold in search of your first big break. And agents, managers, and producers get a dozen query messages each day from people they do not know. Clearly, they cannot read everybody's script in search of that literary needle in the haystack. You need to entice them into wanting to read your screenplay, and you must do so quickly. Not in minutes, but in seconds. That's why you need a scintillating logline.

Construction of a logline is quite mechanical. Start with the hero (protagonist) of your movie, add what he or she does (plot), and finish with why your film is different (twist or hook) from all others of this genre.

Protagonist + Plot + Twist

It should be one sentence if possible, written in present tense. Use descriptive adjectives and keep the sentence tight. Every word must count. Make sure the genre is clear by the way you phrase your sentence. If it's not, begin with "A comedy about . . ." or "A sci-fi tale about . . ." In addition, don't use character names. No one reading your logline will know who Bill or Jane or Michael is. Identify your protagonist by what he or she is, or does (e.g., a lonely schoolteacher . . . a troubled teen . . . a beautiful heiress . . . etc.).

Look at the loglines of the following films and see how they follow the pattern above. Can you identify these movies based on their loglines?

1) A shy boy bonds with an extraterrestrial who's been stranded on earth and disobeys the authorities in order to help the alien contact his spaceship and return home. (*E.T.*)

2) A down and out club boxer is offered a chance to fight for the heavyweight championship but must first learn to see himself as a winner before he can step into the ring. (*Rocky*)

3) After a stint in a mental hospital, a volatile young man moves in with his parents and, while trying to win back his wife, meets a woman who's as unstable as he is—and might just be his perfect match. (*Silver Linings Playbook*)

4) An adventurous archaeologist races around the world to single-handedly prevent the Nazis from turning the greatest archaeological relic of all time into a weapon of world conquest. (*Raiders of the Lost Ark*)

5) A 1940s New York Mafia family struggles to protect their empire as the leadership switches from the aging father to his youngest son, and to new ways of doing business. (*The Godfather*)

6) A lonely writer in a futuristic world falls in love with the "sexy" advanced computer operating system he bought to help run his life, and now can't free himself from his obsession. (*Her*)

7) A man in a troubled marriage finds himself caught in a media frenzy after becoming a prime suspect in his wife's disappearance. (*Gone Girl*)

8) A fur trapper in 1820s America seeks revenge against his fellow trappers, who leave him for dead after he gets mauled by a bear. (*The Revenant*)

9) A German bounty hunter and a sharpshooting freed slave join forces to catch bail-jumpers before undertaking their biggest mission—freeing the slave's wife from a sadistic plantation owner. (*Django Unchained*)

10) A young man and woman from different social classes fall in love aboard an ill-fated voyage at sea. (*Titanic*)

And then there are my stories:

Modern Girls: Two lovable college girls, thrown out of school, join a fraternity dressed as guys and expose male rites of passage.

Cruise Control: A group of parking valets race around town in their guests' luxury cars as they try to win an annual race and return the vehicles back on time without being discovered.

Big Bundle of Joy: A liberal, upper-class, middle-aged couple, afraid of missing out on parenthood, adopt a child from a third world nation who turns out to be a huge sixteen-year-old African boy bent on becoming an American teenager.

Okay, let's say you've come up with a great logline for your movie. You're not done yet, for the logline is just a tease—a sales tool to get someone interested in finding out more about your script. You then need to deliver a great "add-on" which should be included after your logline when contacting someone about your script.

For example, here's the logline for the movie *Rain Man*:

A young, selfish entrepreneur returns home for his father's funeral and learns the entire family fortune has gone to an older autistic brother he never knew he had.

This puts questions in the reader's mind. Who is this entrepreneur? What kind of relationship did he have with his father? Why didn't he know he had an older brother? Tell me more!!! You would follow this up with the add-on that describes, in another sentence or two, a bit more of the actual plot and what we will see on-screen. The add-on for *Rain Man* would be:

> *The entrepreneur kidnaps this older brother and drives him across the country, hoping to befriend him and gain control of the family money. While on the trip, the brother's autism ignites a fraternal connection and reveals a powerful childhood secret that changes their entire relationship.*

This would hopefully be enough to get someone to ask for the script to read. How about an add-on for *Rocky*?

> *The boxer trains hard and, with the help of his long-time manager and adoring new girlfriend, gains the confidence to battle the champ till the final round.*

With a solid logline and add-on you greatly increase the chances that a producer or agent will be so intrigued that they will request to see your script. But that still requires a large time commitment on their part. They may first ask to see a treatment, which is a detailed synopsis of your entire movie. Before you can write that, you need to know all of the main plot points in your story, and in order to know that, you need to understand the structure of a feature film.

STRUCTURE, STRUCTURE, STRUCTURE

Solid structure is by far the most important aspect of a screenplay. Unfortunately, many writers tackling their first script are clueless to this notion. They simply start writing at page one and plow through their story without planning things out beforehand. And guess what? Their scripts are a mess. Crucial plot points occur too early or too late, characters are introduced at the wrong time, and subplots are not incorporated properly. In fact, learning proper structure is so vital to the writing process that on the day I teach this lesson to my college class, I tell them the only excuse for being absent is full-scale Armageddon.

Unlike a novel, whose length can be a hundred pages or seven hundred pages or anywhere in between, a feature script must have a certain page-count range in order for the movie to fall into a 90- to 120-minute timeframe. Any shorter and your film might have trouble finding distribution. Any longer and your name better be James Cameron. The reason movies seldom go beyond two hours is threefold: 1) higher production costs, 2) limited attention span of an audience, and 3) fewer possible screenings per day. A lengthy film may only be able to be shown four times a day instead of five, and that means less box office revenue for the production company and less popcorn sold for the theater owner. Plus, if a film is critically panned, the studio wants as many people as possible to see it opening weekend before word gets out to avoid this smoking turkey.

For a feature to fall under two hours, the script should be between 100 and 120 pages. This is especially important when shopping a spec script. Any fewer pages and the script will appear thin. Any more and it will look like it needs editing. And be aware—agents, producers, and executives take home a dozen scripts every weekend to read, and they all glance at that last page before getting started. A 102-page script will put a smile on their faces. A 127-page script will get them snarling before they see the first Fade In. It's always best to put the reader in a good mood when they're about to judge your material.

I knew nothing about structure when I first started writing. Though I did manage to option one of my early screenplays, I was informed by the producer that my Act 1 break occurred on page 67 of a 110-page script. That's probably why I was quickly replaced as the writer of the movie, despite my objections. And as often happens in the film business, the guy who rewrote me bastardized the script so badly that the production company abandoned the project. A moral victory that cost me a lot of money. I learned the hard way that screenplay structure must be thought through before any actual writing takes place. This will keep the script from meandering and prevent any unnecessary rewriting down the line—especially by someone other than you.

THREE ACTS

The most commonly accepted structure of a screenplay is one that is broken down into three acts. Act 1 is the introduction, Act 2 the obstacles, Act 3 the final outcome. The first and third acts are each about 25 percent of the script, while the second act makes up 50 percent. This enables the screenplay to contain five key plot points, each of which must fall at appropriate timeframes in the film to escalate stakes, increase drama (or laughter), and deliver surprises or suspense. These plot points (PP) help maintain a pace to ensure the audience will be riveted until the lights come on. And it's important to figure out these plot points *before* you do any writing.

Consider this analogy: Your movie is a map of the United States. It begins in Los Angeles and ends in New York City. Without knowing your main plot points ahead of time, you just start driving. Maybe you go to Arizona first, then up to Wyoming, south to Kansas, into Mississippi, up to Ohio, down to North Carolina, and finally north to New York.

You have no itinerary so you're driving all over the place in a haphazard fashion with no notion of where you'll go next. This is not how you want to write your script. But let's say you make plans to drive though five linear destinations along the route. You know you will hit Las Vegas, then Denver, then St. Louis, then Louisville, then Pittsburgh, and on to New York.

This is a much more direct and tighter route. Sure, you may wander a bit between the cities should inspiration suddenly hit you, but you'll never stray totally off course. Your script should be constructed in the same manner. But instead of cities, we will hit a series of five major plot points. Each one occurs at a specific timeframe in the script with a specific purpose in terms of moving the story along.

The following chart is based on a 100-page screenplay. If your script is 110 pages, just add 10 percent to these numbers and adjust accordingly. And please note, these are all approximate page numbers. Nothing is set in stone (except your epitaph).

ACT 1 (Introduction)		ACT 2 (Obstacles)		ACT 3 (Final Outcome)
PP 1	PP 2	PP 3	PP 4	PP 5
(p. 10)	(p. 25)	(p. 50)	(p. 75)	(p. 95)
(Opportunity)	(Goal of Hero)	(No Going Back)	(Big Setback)	(Resolution)

PLOT POINTS

Plot point 1 (Opportunity) takes place about ten minutes into the film, though it could be earlier. It is an important, though often subtle, event involving the protagonist, and the audience may not realize just how important when they first see it. However, without it, the protagonist would not be able to proceed with his ultimate objective in the movie.

Plot point 2 (Goal of Hero) is also the Act 1 break. This is what your hero wants to achieve by the end of the movie. It is what the movie is ultimately about—catching the killer, winning over the girl, blowing up the meteor, etc. Plot point 2 takes place about a quarter of the way through the film.

Plot point 3 (No Going Back) puts reaching that goal further and further in jeopardy. It takes place at the midpoint of the movie, when the protagonist is firmly committed to her goal and faces something unwanted or unexpected that she must overcome.

Plot point 4 (Big Setback), the Act 2 break, takes place three quarters of the way through the film and presents the protagonist's greatest challenge, one that is so daunting it becomes her lowest point in the film, when it looks like she will fail to achieve the goal set in plot point 2.

Plot point 5 (Resolution) is the victory she claims when she overcomes the obstacles and achieves her goal. It is one of the final scenes of the movie, if not the last.

STAGES

Before, between, and after these major plot points are the various stages of the movie. And just like with the plot points, each stage has a purpose in moving along the story.

ACT 1		ACT 2		ACT 3	
(Setup)	(Moving Forward)	(Progress)	(Complications)	(Final Drive)	(Wrap-up)
PP 1	PP 2	PP 3	PP 4	PP 5	
(p. 10)	(p. 25)	(p. 50)	(p. 75)	(p. 95)	

Stage 1 (Setup) is the opening of the script. It lasts about ten pages and introduces us to the protagonist, sets the tone and genre of the film, and puts the movie in motion.

Stage 2 (Moving Forward), which occurs between plot points 1 and 2, sends the protagonist on his journey, though his ultimate goal has not yet been established. So far everything is going well.

Stage 3 (Progress) is when the protagonist is actively trying to achieve his goal. There are obstacles, but nothing he can't overcome.

Stage 4 (Complications) is when the obstacles become much more difficult, the stakes have been raised, and things aren't looking too promising for our hero.

Stage 5 (Final Drive) is when the protagonist figures out a way to make one last ditch effort to achieve his goal. As bad as things look, he's not giving up.

Stage 6 (Wrap-up) is when the story is over, subplots are resolved, and the characters reflect on their accomplishments.

Here is a movie broken down into all of its structural elements:

ACT I
STAGE I: SETUP (PAGES I–I0)

a) **Draw the reader into the story.** Make the opening visual and dynamic.

b) **Reveal the everyday life of the protagonist.** How does the hero start out?

c) **Establish the personality of the hero.** Is he funny, likable, powerful, dumb, etc.?

PLOT POINT I: OPPORTUNITY, BY PAGE I0.

a) Protagonist is presented with an important event that will pay off later.

b) It is not the specific goal of the hero, or what the movie is ultimately about.

STAGE 2: MOVING FORWARD (PAGES I0–25)

a) The protagonist reacts to the new situation that resulted from the opportunity.

b) He gets acclimated to any new surroundings and formulates a specific plan.

c) He enters this stage willingly, with excitement and anticipation.

PLOT POINT 2: GOAL OF HERO. PAGE 25. ACT I BREAK.

a) Protagonist has a clear goal in mind of what he needs to achieve by the end of the film.

b) It is what the movie is ultimately about.

ACT 2

STAGE 3: PROGRESS (PAGES 25–50)

a) The protagonist is moving forward as he takes action to achieve his goal.

b) He faces some obstacles, but is able to overcome them.

PLOT POINT 3: NO GOING BACK. PAGE 50.

a) The protagonist is fully committed to attaining his goal. There's no turning back.

b) He is more involved with other characters and is taking greater risks.

STAGE 4: COMPLICATIONS (PAGES 50–75)

a) The protagonist's ability to achieve his goal becomes far more difficult.

b) He has much more to lose if he fails.

c) The conflicts become greater and greater.

PLOT POINT 4: BIG SETBACK. PAGE 75. ACT 2 BREAK.

a) It seems that all is lost for the protagonist. It is unlikely he will achieve his goal.

b) The only option is to make one last all-or-nothing effort.

ACT 3
STAGE 5: FINAL DRIVE (PAGES 75–95)

a) The conflict becomes overwhelming and the pace is accelerated.

b) Though everything is working against the protagonist, he charges forward.

PLOT POINT 5: RESOLUTION. PAGE 95.

a) The protagonist overcomes all obstacles and achieves his goal.

b) He must do it on his own and determine his own fate.

STAGE 6: WRAP-UP (PAGES 95–100)

a) The protagonist reflects on achieving his objective.

b) All open subplot stories are resolved.

c) Clues for a sequel may be put in place.

Remember, the most important thing for you to do as a writer is to come up with your five major plot points before you ever start writing. This breaks down the script into smaller sections and lets you know what you have to accomplish between each of these plot points. Let's look at the various major plot points of some well-known movies. Some of these films are longer than ninety minutes and hence their stages will last longer and the plot points will occur later than in the hundred-page model. They are all classics so if you haven't seen them, shame, shame, shame. But don't fret. Stream them, go to the library, or rent the DVD.

THE GODFATHER

PP1) Michael Corleone (Al Pacino), not yet a part of the family business, finds out his father, Vito Corleone (Marlon Brando), has been shot.

PP2) Seeking revenge, Michael kills a rival mob boss and a dirty cop in a restaurant. A wanted man, he must leave the country. Will he ever get back together with his family and become the successful individual he set out to be? This is the goal of the movie that needs to be resolved.

PP3) Having fled to Sicily, Michael is losing touch with his family.

PP4) After Michael's brother Sonny (James Caan) is gunned down at a toll booth, his new wife is killed by a car bomb. This is Michael's lowest point.

PP5) Michael returns home and takes over the family business when his father dies from natural causes. He is the most ruthless godfather ever.

THE VERDICT

PP1) Lawyer Frank Galvin (Paul Newman) is given a simple, but lucrative, malpractice case to settle.

PP2) Instead of taking a large settlement offer, his conscience gets the best of him and he elects to try the case instead without even telling the plaintiffs. Will he win? That is the goal that must be resolved.

PP3) Frank's witnesses disappear. He tries to delay the case but the judge refuses.

PP4) Frank realizes he has no concrete evidence and is going to lose the case. His lowest point.

PP5) The most important witness makes a surprise appearance in court and the jury wants to award the plaintiff an even bigger settlement.

NORTH BY NORTHWEST

PP1) Roger Thornhill (Cary Grant) is kidnapped while being mistaken for an elusive spy.

PP2) Trying to figure out what is going on, Roger ends up at the United Nations and is accused of stabbing a diplomat. On the lam, he knows he must clear his name before he gets arrested and figure out what's going on. That's his goal.

PP3) Roger is nearly gunned down in a cornfield, sent there by Eve (Eva Marie Saint), a woman he met on a train and a romantic interest. He now knows she's working for the bad guys.

PP4) Roger finds out Eve is actually an undercover spy for the U.S. government. But when he tries to convince her to leave her dangerous assignment, he is knocked out and locked in a room by her superiors. His lowest point.

PP5) Roger escapes and rescues Eve on the faces of Mount Rushmore.

A great exercise for you is to watch one of your favorite movies and as you do, make a list on a legal pad or on your computer of each scene, marking every ten minutes of the film. Can you identify the major plot points? Do they occur at the proper timeframes of the story? Almost every movie follows this structure, whether you are aware of it or not. Once you have your main plot points set, you can move to the next step in writing the script. It may be a step outline, or it may be a treatment. Let's talk about each.

PROPER TREATMENTS

A treatment is a well-developed synopsis of your movie. It's more than one page (that would simply *be* a synopsis) but less than ten. Five or six pages is ideal, single-spaced, broken down into separate paragraphs. That's long enough to reveal what is happening in your story, but short enough to be read in about ten minutes.

Treatments are not written like short stories. There is almost no dialogue and the descriptions are simple, direct, and fact-based. The amount of space devoted to each act is very different than it will be in the screenplay itself. You may spend more than 25 percent of your treatment page count on Act 1 in order to effectively introduce all of your characters and get the story in motion, and less than 50 percent on Act 2, where the story can now be advanced more succinctly. You might also leave out some of the details of your subplots so as not to overemphasize their importance. Act 3 is often short, merely wrapping up and resolving the story.

There are several good reasons to write a treatment once you've figured out your major plot points. There are also several good reasons to *not* write a treatment and go directly from your plot points to a step outline. Let me elaborate:

REASONS TO WRITE A TREATMENT

1) **It will help you flesh out your story.** Even after you've come up with the five main plot points, there are still many other plot points needed to keep the story moving forward. The more you can come up with, the easier it will be to connect the dots of your story. Yes, you can do this in an outline, but forcing yourself to write out the entire movie in a more general form enables you to really see how your acts are going to develop and whether or not you have a complete story. You don't have to come up with specific scenes, but simply the general flow of the film, as if you were pitching it to someone. Is there too much setup? Is the second act thin? Do you have a satisfying ending? These questions will be answered as you write the treatment.

2) **People may ask to see a treatment.** You might query an agent, manager, or producer in hopes of getting them to read your script. They may find your logline to be intriguing, but not yet be prepared to invest over an hour of their time reading the screenplay of someone

they don't know. (Remember, most scripts from novice writers are dismal . . . and that's being kind.) However, these industry people may be willing to give you ten minutes of their time to read through your story to see if they feel a captivating movie is really there. If they like the treatment, they will hopefully then ask to read the entire script. It's not ideal. You'd much rather they read the script right off the bat. But right now, at this point in your career, they're calling the shots. Be thankful they at least see enough potential in your premise to want to read something. (Hey, be thankful they even got back to you at all.) And a treatment is better than having them request a one-page synopsis, which may happen as well. When someone in the industry does ask for a treatment, you want to be able to send it to them that day. If you don't have one prepared, it may take several days or longer to write one. By the time you email it to the person requesting it, they may have already forgotten who you are.

3) **You can use it as a leave-behind.** You've just spent fifteen minutes pitching your movie idea to a studio executive. Problem is, that executive cannot hire you to write the script. He needs to get the approval of the studio president and will first re-pitch the idea at a creative meeting. Do you trust him to retell your story with the same enthusiasm you told it? Might he leave out

important details, or mess up the timing of some key plot points? Leaving him a written treatment after your meeting gives him a tool to refer to when trying to sell your story to the powers that be. Be aware, however, that this leave-behind can also work against you. Sometimes the executive may simply pass the treatment on to the studio president and co-workers without a proper retelling of the story at all. And, as I'll discuss in a moment, a treatment without proper oral accompaniment can be much worse than no treatment at all.

4) **You can use your treatment to register your story with the Writers Guild of America (WGA).** Many writers are afraid that someone is going to steal their brilliant idea. And many of these same scribes will go to their graves with that brilliant idea safely locked away because they never felt secure enough to let anyone else hear it. Well, don't lose a potential sale because of your paranoia. Legitimate members of the entertainment industry are in business to buy ideas, not steal them. If you have something they desire, they have the money to pay you for it. This doesn't mean there aren't unscrupulous elements in the movie business who may swipe a good idea. That's why you need to know who you're sending your material to. Are they an established entity in the community? Have they produced movies before? Do they work for a respected company?

Do a little research before you send query messages to anybody who calls themselves a producer. And protect your material before sending it out.

The preferred way for most companies is for you to register your script with the Writers Guild. Simply go online to wga.org and follow the prompts for Registration. It costs $20 for nonmembers. You can register treatments, movie scripts, TV scripts, outlines, novels, poems, drawings, music, whatever you want. Heck, you can register your grandma's meatloaf recipe if you desire. What the registration does is to give you a date that establishes when you created said material should issues arise in the future. The downside is that this registration only lasts for five years and then has to be renewed. As an alternative, you can protect your work through the U.S. Copyright Office as well. More about registration later on when I talk about the WGA.

While these are all good reasons to write a treatment, there are several equally good reasons why you should not. In fact, most professional writers do not write treatments but rather go directly from premise to plot points to the step outline stage.

REASONS *NOT* TO WRITE A TREATMENT

1) **It will be considered incomplete.** How do you condense a 110-page screenplay into five or six pages? You can't! If

you focus on the characters, the plot may become unclear. If you focus on the plot, the characters might come off as thin. If you do figure out a way to do both, the tone or theme may be hazy. Comedies may rely on witty banter that won't be present in a treatment. Elaborate action scenes with high-stakes stunts and drama will be shortchanged as well. And if you do try to put in absolutely everything, your treatment will be twenty pages long. A person could have read half of the actual script by the time he gets through reading all that.

2) **It will be misinterpreted.** Remember, a screenplay is a blueprint for a movie. The reader has to be able to visualize all the descriptions, hear the actors performing the lines, imagine what the camera angles might be, sense the type of music that will be present. It's hard enough to convey everything that will be seen or heard on-screen through a screenplay. A treatment is one step further removed from the final product than the script. It takes an imaginative, thoughtful reader to be able to envision what the movie will be like. And not all readers are that.

3) **It will be taken as fact.** Even worse than misinterpreting the treatment is a reader who thinks everything you've written will end up in the script. What if you get new ideas while writing? What if you have subplots that you leave out of the treatment because you don't

want them to compete with your main story? When they read the script and see all this new material, they may ask, "Where'd that come from? It wasn't in the treatment."

4) **It delays the writing process.** It may take you a week or two to write your treatment. Then you need to go over it, make changes, rewrite, polish it, etc. The time it takes to do all this could be better spent on your outline and the writing of the actual script. Remember, you're not trying to sell a treatment. You're trying to sell a screenplay, so that's where your energies should be focused.

5) **Someone will love it.** If they do, your script better be an accurate portrayal of what they expect to see. When you change things and fill in the holes, you open yourself up for not delivering what was expected. This also puts a lot of pressure on you to hit one out of the park with your script.

Here is a sample of a treatment I wrote years ago for a script entitled *Smitten* that I later optioned. The logline is: A cheating husband gives his socially awkward teenage son advice on how to pursue a woman, only to have it all come back and haunt him when the girl his son has fallen for turns out to be his dad's own young mistress.

I'm sure you will find many holes that were later filled in during the screenwriting process.

SMITTEN

ACT 1

MARTY POWELL, age fifteen, is a bright, precocious loner who attends Yardley Academy, a prestigious private high school on the Upper East Side of Manhattan. We first meet him stuck upside down in a toilet in the boys' bathroom, legs held upright by two custodians trying to extricate him as he dangles perilously close to sea level. Marty's parents, GORDON and BLANCHE, have been summoned to retrieve him by MR. PETERSON, the old and ornery school headmaster, and Gordon is none too happy about this disruption to his day.

We learn that Marty has been kicked out of three schools in five years for a number of transgressions ranging from fighting with the school bullies to failing courses. Though always on the losing end of any physical confrontation due to his diminutive stature, Marty is a champion when it comes to scathing wit, and this often gets him in trouble. Gordon, a successful sports agent and former pro athlete, can't understand the lad's antisocial behavior, especially as his other son, James, seems so perfect a boy. Gordon has tried everything to correct Marty's errant ways, but has only succeeded in increasing the tension between the two.

While in the boys' bathroom, Marty's parents learn that their son got into an altercation with the school bully, Pinky Romero, erroneously praised as a model student by headmaster Peterson. Seems Pinky tried to convince Marty to join his club, and Marty refused. Gordon can't believe his son turned down an opportunity to partake in an extracurricular activity, and orders Marty to join—until he finds out the club is the Young Nazis for Christ. "Ingrates . . . all of them," is all Gordon can say as he rushes off back to work.

We next see a reluctant Gordon being escorted through a tenement apartment building by CARO-LINE, a stunning young woman in her early twenties. She wants him to meet her friend, MARIA, a pregnant Hispanic woman who lives with her tattoo-laden brother, RAUL. They are having problems with their landlord, who has failed to make necessary repairs. Caroline wants Gordon to contact the building owner and threaten him with legal action. Gordon informs her that he is a sports attorney, not a legal clinic, and blames the tenants for their own problems, saying one risks their life just entering the building. But dying to get out of there, he agrees to do what he can. As they head off, Gordon gives Caroline a gift box. She opens it to find a sexy negligee. As they surreptitiously kiss, we realize they are having an affair.

That weekend, we meet Marty's brother, JAMES, age seventeen, a handsome, athletic, all-American boy. He also drinks excessively and smokes pot, unbeknownst to his proud father. James thinks Marty is weird, and though they share a bedroom, the two boys do what they can to avoid each other. Gordon is about to head off to play golf with his wife, but Blanche, an ad executive, informs him she has to go into the office to catch up on some work. He is livid, feeling that ever since she took that job she's been spending less and less time doing the things he wants to do. She tells him her workload will lighten up soon and heads off.

Gordon realizes this might be a good time to call Caroline, and he slips into a hall closet to make the call. While in there, Marty comes down the stairs and bids him adieu. Embarrassed, Gordon leaps out and tells Marty they need to talk. Marty says he needs to meet his friend Alvin, but an impatient Gordon tells him that can wait. Gordon tries to talk to Marty about taking on more adult responsibilities and being more like his brother, but Marty keeps goofing on him. Finally, Gordon can't take it anymore and sends him on his way.

Marty and ALVIN, a portly school chum, head uptown on their bikes. Marty knows his dad is cheating on his mom and tells Alvin they are heading to the home of the mistress. He found a receipt from Victoria's Secret in his father's coat pocket. Written on it is: Maria Espinoza, Paradise Arms Apts., with an address. Marty says he's going to leave her an anonymous note saying that Gordon is a married ex-con with six kids, three other girlfriends, and two social diseases. He wants to save his parents' marriage and if that note won't do it, nothing will. But when Alvin finds out the building is in Spanish Harlem, he races off. "Even the cops won't go there."

Caroline is at Maria's home, helping her fill out some legal forms that Gordon gave her, when Marty tries to slip the note under the door. Maria notices and opens the door. Marty, on the other side, gazes at her pregnant belly. "Maria?" he asks nervously. "Yes," she responds. Marty is so shook up at who he thinks his father's mistress is that he simply says, "Wrong address," and runs off. Caroline says goodbye to Maria and leaves. She spots Marty unchaining his bike and asks him if he can give her a lift as cabs don't come to this neighborhood very often. He is confused as all he has is his bike, but she tells him not to worry, she can sit on the handlebars.

The two head back downtown, Marty staring at her sexy bottom as he pedals. He slyly asks her about Maria and finds out that she and Maria work together for a veterinarian. Apparently, Maria's boyfriend, an older guy, promised her the world and then ran off, leaving her seven months pregnant and hurting for cash. Caroline says she thinks the guy is actually married and never told her. Marty is aghast and thinks this sounds like something his father would do. He drops her off at her apartment and says goodbye, vowing to himself to seek justice.

ACT 2

Blanche, at work, is hit on by RICHARD, her sleazy young assistant. She informs him in no uncertain terms that she is happily married and that he is not that much older than her oldest son. Plus, he's engaged. Absolutely not interested.

WALTER SUTTON, age twenty-one, a gentle 6'9" giant and the NBA's recent number one draft pick, stops by the Powell house with his cousin, JEROME. Walter is Gordon's biggest client ever and is returning the keys to the car he and Jerome borrowed to pick up Jerome's girlfriend at the airport. They find Marty at home eating lunch because Pinky stole his lunch money. As Jerome writes a note—"Gordon, thanks, you are the greatest. Love ya, baby. Jerome"—Walter tells Marty that when he was fifteen he was bullied too. Marty is shocked and wants to know by whom: King Kong and Godzilla?

Walter laughs and tells him he was a skinny kid back then and was picked on too. Never even thought about pro ball. Wanted to be a doctor. Marty asks if he fought the bullies. Walter says that fighting never solved anything. He got together some friends, challenged them to a game of hoops, and whipped their butts in front of everyone. They didn't have much to say after that. Marty says that he's not good at sports and challenging Pinky to a spelling bee wouldn't be the same.

Walter laughs and knows that the lad will figure something out.

Caroline and Gordon take a stroll through the Central Park Zoo. She is upset because she doesn't think their relationship will go anywhere. Gordon assures her that's not the case. He plans to tell Blanche that he is leaving her as soon as the right moment arises. While at the zoo, Caroline notices a baby llama being fed a hot dog by some schoolkids. She wants to do something about this abuse but Gordon quickly scoots her away.

While on the playground at Yardley Academy, Marty tells Alvin about meeting Maria and that he intends to make sure his dad takes responsibility for her predicament. He also tells him about sexy Caroline and, since he knows where she lives, can talk to her to find out if his dad takes any action. We also meet PAMELA, a schoolgirl who has a crush on Marty, and PINKY and his gang, who start to bully Marty. They threaten to slam him into the toilet again, but Marty flings a cup of soda into Pinky's face and hightails it. While fleeing, he crashes into headmaster Peterson, who looks at him with contempt as Pinky kindly helps the old man up.

That night at dinner, Gordon tells Marty how he had to beg Peterson to let him finish the semester. In the background, Marty has put on the song "How Do You Solve a Problem Like Maria?" from *The Sound of Music*. He tries to gauge his dad's reaction but gets none. That evening, Gordon talks to Caroline on the phone. Apparently, she wants to borrow his car but he refuses and tells her not to call him when he's at home. Blanche overhears the conversation and is aghast at the possibility that her husband might be having an affair.

That night, Marty and Alvin head over to Caroline's apartment. When they get there, she is running out and tells the boys she needs their help. They all hop into an SUV borrowed from Maria's brother and head to the zoo. Climbing a fence, she kidnaps the baby llama and takes it back to her place. Alvin is so terrified he runs home. Once inside Caroline's apartment, the two talk about old movies and end up watching a romantic one together. She asks him why she can't ever meet a nice sweet guy. Marty, meanwhile, is quite excited about being near her and has a big crush. As they continue watching the film, both doze off. When Marty wakes up, he realizes it is 12:30 A.M. and he needs to get home. He asks about Maria and races off.

Gordon and Blanche are getting ready for bed. She looks over some bills online, still stunned from the earlier overheard phone call. Gordon talks about a trip to the mountains that he's planned, and makes a big deal about giving up valuable negotiating time over Walter's contract, simply because she wants to go. He thinks she should be more grateful at this sacrifice of his. Blanche says she needs to tie up some loose "affairs," looking for his reaction. She also notices a charge from a florist on a credit card statement. Then they hear noise out in the hall. It is Marty coming back from Caroline's. At first Gordon is furious, but Marty tells him he was out with a friend. When Gordon figures out it was a "girl" friend, he's proud of his son. Maybe he's starting to get his life in order. Regardless, Blanche grounds him for being out so late.

Gordon, Marty, and Walter head down Fifth Avenue toward a jewelry store. They pass a newsstand with a headline: "Llama still missing from zoo." Gordon tells Walter that Marty has a girlfriend. In the store, Walter picks up a beautiful engagement ring. The jeweler also tells Gordon he has the bracelet he ordered and shows it to him. Gordon quickly tells him he'll pick it up later. Walter gives Marty some sincere advice about love. As they drive home, Marty puts an oldies album into the CD player. The '70s hit "Take a Letter Maria" starts playing. Still no reaction from Gordon. Marty asks his father the difference between like and love. Gordon tells him that to show someone you love them, you must give them things like flowers and candy. Marty asks him if he loves his mom. Gordon says, "Of course." Marty then asks why he doesn't buy her flowers and candy anymore. Disturbed, Gordon quickly changes the subject.

On the school playground, Marty tells Alvin about his evening with Caroline. He says he plans to see her again. Alvin says he's full of it, but Marty tells him he's going to see her that afternoon. He goes to her building, climbs the fire escape, and breaks into her apartment.

While there, he prepares a spaghetti dinner and sets out flowers he brought her. When she returns home, she is flattered, but informs him that she can't have dinner with him that night. Her boyfriend is coming over. Marty never realized that she might be seeing someone. And by the knock on the door, it appears he has just arrived. Embarrassed and depressed, Marty sneaks back out the window as Gordon enters for an early evening tryst. When he sees the dinner, Caroline tells him a young man made it for her. Gordon is jealous but she responds that he has nothing to worry about.

At the same time, Blanche tries to contact Gordon but he isn't answering his phone. Her assistant, Richard, insinuates that maybe he is up to some hanky-panky. She refutes his suggestion and pushes him out of her office. As she looks through some paperwork, she finds a strange note. It's the one that Jerome left earlier, which apparently got mixed in with her files. "Love ya baby, Jerome"?! My god, he's not only having an affair, worries Blanche. He's having a gay affair.

Later that evening, Gordon discovers the llama hidden in Caroline's apartment. He is furious at her and wants to know how she got it. She tells him a friend helped her. Then he discovers the flowers Marty brought over and is more jealous than ever.

Back at the Yardley playground, Marty and Alvin talk more about Caroline. That is, until Pinky heads over. He's ready to smash Marty's head, but Marty takes the

advice of Walter and tells him fighting never solved anything. Pinky laughs and suggests they settle this on the
basketball court instead. Marty's friends against his, loser
pays a hundred bucks to the other team. Marty agrees,
much to the chagrin of Alvin.

Gordon is frantic that he is losing Caroline to some
young stud. Marty, meanwhile, blasts "Maria" from *West
Side Story* on the stereo. Blanche, standoffish, thinks that
must be the name of Marty's new friend.

Gordon and Blanche head out of town for their weekend in the mountains. As soon as they're gone, James
throws a wild party at their home. Unable to take the
noise anymore, Marty heads off toward Caroline's house.
Just as he gets there, he catches her running out. Maria
has just called. Her brother found out where her boyfriend is staying and is going to kill him. Marty runs off
with her, thinking this is about his father.

They get to Maria's apartment. Marty bursts in and
confronts Raul, but there in the apartment is ERNESTO,
an older man holding hands with Maria. This is her boyfriend and he has returned to do the honorable thing and
marry her. Marty is very confused. He and Caroline head
back to her apartment where they discuss relationships
and friendship. They fall asleep in each other's arms.

When Marty wakes up he realizes he is late for school.
He rushes off to Yardley but nods off in class, dreaming
about Caroline. An elderly teacher wakes him and asks
him to come to the blackboard for an assignment. As he

steps forward, he sees her as Caroline and gives her a big kiss. The teacher screams.

Up in the mountains, Gordon, on the golf course, boasts of the huge NBA deal he's going to get for Walter Sutton. It should make him the most respected sports agent in the country. Suddenly he's interrupted by Blanche. Marty's in trouble, they have to leave. Upset, he and Blanche arrive home unexpectedly and find their house in a shambles from James' party. Gordon talks about the importance of family and Blanche questions her husband on it as well. Later, Marty asks his dad for some romantic advice. His dad tells him if you really love someone, you go all out to prove it.

That night, Gordon gives Caroline the bracelet seen earlier at the jewelry store. But then he notices a seashell necklace she's wearing. It fuels his jealously, even though she tells him it was given to her by just a friend. But Gordon thinks, this guy is good. If he wants a fight, he's got one. Marty is spurred on by his father's advice as well, and the two of them shower Caroline with flowers and candy and love notes. Gordon realizes he just can't keep up.

The day of Marty's basketball game with Pinky finally arrives. But it appears Marty's team is short one player. Pinky and friends ridicule him until the fifth player arrives. It is Marty's friend, NBA prospect Walter Sutton. Pinky's team can't believe it, and naturally they get crushed. But Marty lets Pinky off on the bet and settles for a handshake instead.

Meanwhile, Gordon feels he has only one choice. While walking down the street with Caroline, he tells her he's going to leave Blanche. They have an awards show to attend that weekend for Walter. When that's over he's going to break it to her. Suddenly they see a man choking. Walter gives him the Heimlich maneuver which dislodges some food, but the man is shook up. Gordon holds him until he can catch his breath. Passing by in a cab is Blanche. She sees Gordon with his arms around the man and assumes this must be Jerome. In public, no less. How humiliating!

Marty and Caroline give the llama a bath. She takes off her bracelet to get it out of the way. Marty recognizes it from the jewelry store. When she puts it on the counter, he looks at the inscription: "All my love, Gordon." Marty is so devastated at the realization of who Caroline's boyfriend is, he simply heads off without explanation. He runs into Pamela, the girl who has a crush on him, and she tries to make small talk, but he's not feeling it.

That night at the Powell dinner table, Gordon tells his kids that Walter has invited them to attend the awards show that weekend. They can even bring a guest. Gordon suggests that Marty bring his new little girlfriend and Marty grins, devising a plan. Blanche, however, is losing it, convinced now more than ever that Gordon is having a gay affair. When she puts down the salad plates, his uncut cucumber and twin tomatoes have been set in an explicit anatomical arrangement.

ACT 3

The awards show is in the main ballroom of the New York Hilton. When Caroline, Marty's guest, arrives, she is surprised to find out it is an awards show. She is even more surprised when she sees who Marty's father is. And Gordon is just as stunned. They all sit together at a dinner table just prior to the televised show. Blanche is getting drunk and talks to Caroline about knowing what Gordon has been up to. Caroline thinks she's referring to her and offers to leave, but Blanche says it's not her fault and darts off. Gordon catches up to her in a corridor, just as a TV interviewer steps up to him, wanting to talk about Walter. But Gordon is in the midst of his conversation with Blanche, who calls him a two-timing homosexual. This exchange goes out on all the big-screen TVs in the banquet hall. Everybody is shocked. Blanche runs off. Caroline asks Gordon what that was all about, and he has no idea. Then James runs up to his dad, excited. "I'm gay too, dad. I never knew how to tell you. I thought you'd be ashamed. Now we'll have some real things to talk about!"

Caroline realizes it's some misunderstanding but she breaks up with Gordon on account of Marty. Just then, Walter is announced as Amateur Athlete of the Year. When he goes onstage to collect his award, he makes an announcement. Gordon's "coming out" and being true to himself has given him the courage to also be brave—he doesn't want to play pro ball. He wants to be a doctor and is going to go to medical school instead. And he has Gordon to thank. All Gordon can see are the millions in commissions going out the window. Marty and Gordon have a real father-son chat and Gordon says he will try to be a better husband and father.

Blanche, meanwhile, has called her assistant to meet her for a drink. Richard leaves his fiancée to meet her, thinking they're going to have a fling. But she fires him instead, saying by putting him in his place today, maybe he won't turn out to be the asshole her husband is.

Gordon and Blanche agree to work on their relationship. He is accepting of James' sexuality. And he agrees to be less critical of Marty. Marty visits Caroline and they agree to stay friends. And he heads off, with Pamela, his new friend.

OUTLINES, STEP BY STEP

A treatment presents a basic narrative of your story, how it will unfold, and the main characters in it. Now it's time to get down into the weeds and create a step outline, also known as a beat sheet. This is critical before starting to write your script, sort of what architectural plans are to a building. Simply put, a step outline is a list of all (or at least a majority of) the scenes in your movie. If you don't create one, you may end up with your Act 1 break on page 67 and immediately get replaced as the writer (see Lesson 4).

In order to make the 25/50/25 percent three-act screenplay structure work, Act 1 and Act 3 should have approximately fourteen scenes each, while Act 2 would have double, or twenty-eight. Again, these numbers are not exact, but if your first act has only six scenes, it's probably too short. If it has twenty-two, it's most likely too long. A scene is defined as any time you have a new scene heading (INT. GARAGE – DAY) in your script. Some scenes may only be a quarter of a page long, others could run three or four pages. And don't confuse a sequence with a scene. A sequence is a group of related scenes that come one after the other. For example, you might have the "hospital" sequence in your script, made up of seven continuous scenes:

1) A man gets in a car crash.

2) He is driven to the hospital in an ambulance.

3) Doctors treat him into the emergency room.

4) A nurse calls his wife.

5) The man is wheeled into surgery.

6) The wife arrives at the hospital.

7) The doctor informs her of his status.

Each one of these counts as a scene since they take place in new locations. Together, they make up one sequence.

Be aware, you're not going to know every scene in your movie before you start writing the script. You will probably know most of Act 1, but the other acts may be less developed at the start. That is fine. If you know half of the twenty-eight scenes in Act 2, you know enough to keep going. The rest will fill in as you come up with more ideas and further develop your subplots.

The amount of information you put in a step outline is usually brief, as it's a personal tool generally not shared with producers, directors, or executives working with you on your project. Simply list the scene number, followed by its location, followed by a sentence or two of what happens and is said in that scene. It does not have specific dialogue, but you do want to know what the characters are talking about. For instance:

1) COFFEE HOUSE—Pam and Sue discuss Sally's pregnancy.

This may be all you need to say. The same is true for action:

2) HIGHWAY—Car chase, Ted and Bob.

You'll get into the details when you write the script. How you organize the outline also differs with each writer. Some like to write each scene on an index card and then put them in order on a table or tacked to a bulletin board. I find this to be problematic as it always means shuffling around all the cards when you want to add, delete, and switch the order of a scene. Other writers simply list them on their computers and add, delete, and move them around accordingly. (There is specific software that can help you do this, which I will discuss later in the software lesson.) Personally, I prefer to handwrite every scene on a line on a legal pad so I can sit back in a chair and follow the movie's progression with a quick downturn of my eyes. If I want to delete a scene, I cross it out. If I want to add one, I write it on the right side of the pad and draw it in with an arrow. When the page gets too messy to read, I redo a fresh copy and start the list again. Yes, I know, this sounds archaic in the high-tech world we live in today. But I also remember when "pre-owned" vehicles were called used cars, "sick" meant you were bedridden, and "hook-up" was what you did to your TV if you wanted to get cable, so I'm a little jaded in the ways of old.

Here is a step outline of Act 1 for the 1991 movie *Thelma & Louise,* written by Callie Khouri, for which she won the Academy Award for Best Original Screenplay. In my class, we watch the first act and review the step outline. Even if you don't remember the film, you can see how the beat sheet looks.

THELMA & LOUISE (ACT 1)

1. DINER—Louise works as waitress at diner.

2. DINER/KITCHEN—Phone call between Louise & Thelma. Discuss getting out of town for weekend camping trip. Thelma doesn't tell husband Darryl her plans.

3. OUTSIDE THELMA'S HOUSE—Darryl heads off to work.

4. DINER/KITCHEN—Phone call between Louise & Thelma. Thelma says she's going on trip.

5. OUTSIDE DINER—Louise gets in car after work.

6. THELMA'S BEDROOM—Thelma overpacks for trip. Stashes gun in suitcase.

7. LOUISE'S BEDROOM—Louise packs like an Eagle Scout. Calls boyfriend Jimmy on phone. No answer.

8. THELMA'S HOUSE—Louise picks up Thelma for trip.

9. CAR ON INTERSTATE—Thelma gives Louise gun. Says she didn't tell Darryl she was leaving.

10. CAR ON COUNTRY ROAD—Thelma and Louise decide to stop for food.

11. SILVER BULLET CLUB—Bar, pool tables, band. Ladies order drinks. Jimmy hasn't called Louise. Harlan hits on ladies.

12. CLUB (LATER)—Drunk Thelma dances with Harlan.

13. CLUB RESTROOM—Louise fixes her makeup in mirror.

14. CLUB PARKING LOT—Harlan puts moves on ill Thelma, tries to rape her. Louise tells him to stop. He ticks her off. She shoots him. Ladies flee.

Plot point 2 (Act 1 break) is obvious. The ladies have just killed a man in the club's parking lot. Will they turn themselves in? Will they claim self-defense? Will they run? How will they avoid going to prison for murder? This is now the goal of our protagonists and the thing that needs to be resolved by the end of the film. What is plot point 1, the opportunity? If you've watched the movie, it's when Thelma gives Louise her gun. Without it, there would be no killing. And if Louise just pulled out a gun from her purse without any setup, you'd be asking yourself, "Where the heck did that gun come from? How convenient!"

As with examining structure, a great exercise is to pick

one of your favorite movies and reverse engineer a step outline as you watch it. Simply write down one sentence about
what is going on in each scene on a pad or on your computer. Keep track of the running time as well and mark what
scene occurs every ten minutes of the film. Then look it over.
Can you identify all the major plot points? Do they fall in
the appropriate timeframes of the movie? How are the subplots interspersed within the main plot? Coming up with a
detailed step outline for your script will make the whole
writing process a lot easier.

QUITE A CHARACTER

The best story in the world will appear thin and uninspired if you don't create real, unique, and lively characters. Who can forget Forrest Gump, Dirty Harry, Jack Sparrow, Scarlett O'Hara, or Buzz Lightyear? All had distinct personalities with unforgettable traits. But before you create your memorable characters, you need to remember that they all have two lives: before and after. The "before" life is the character's backstory. That is everything that has happened to her from birth to the start of the movie. The "after" life is everything that happens from the time she first appears on-screen to the end of the film. A writer needs to know the "before" life because this will shape the actions she does and the things she says throughout the film. The three main areas you need to know are her social, psychological, and physical attributes.

Social Attributes include a character's education, religion, political views, income, status, hobbies, and affiliations.

Psychological Attributes include things like her passions, fears, needs, morality, intelligence, habits, and any addictions.

Physical Attributes are things like height, weight, looks, athleticism, disabilities, gender, and health.

Not all of these attributes will have a bearing on your movie. Whether your protagonist is a Baptist or a Catholic may make no difference to your story, nor if she went to a two-year college or a four-year school. But what if she was a Muslim, would it then? What if she was a high school dropout, or had a Ph.D.? What if she was African-American . . . or had a limp . . . or a drinking problem . . . or a fear of flying . . . or was a staunch member of the NRA . . . or cheated on her taxes . . . or was quite beautiful . . . or collected classic art . . . or threw temper tantrums . . . or used to play in the NFL? You could give your character any one of these attributes as her "before" life (okay, maybe not former NFL), which would then affect her actions during her "after" life. These are the things you need to think of before you start developing the character and writing the script.

Interesting characters are well rounded, multidimensional, and, like real people, have likeable qualities so that you care about them, root for them, and can relate to them. But they also need flaws and vulnerabilities to make them intriguing and provide opportunities for them to be challenged along the way. The more rounded your characters are, the more real they will appear. And even bigger-than-life characters need to have flaws. For instance, Superman was vulnerable to kryptonite (and Lois Lane). And Indiana Jones could not stand those damn snakes. And what is true for your protagonist is equally true for your antagonist. Think of Darth Vader or Nurse Ratched or the Wicked Witch of the West. These characters were really evil, but smart, with specific motives, creating true challenges for their protagonists. And bad guys need to have good qualities too to keep them well rounded. Hannibal Lecter in *The Silence of the Lambs* was a brilliant psychiatrist. He just happened to eat people.

While the protagonist is usually the main character of the movie, antagonists don't always have to be people. A meteor heading to Earth can be an antagonist (*Armageddon*), an animal can (*Jaws*), as can simply fighting the elements while struggling to get back to Earth (*The Martian*). Even a drinking problem or a gambling addiction or an emotional problem that jeopardizes a character's relationship with loved ones can be an antagonist (*Silver Linings Playbook*).

Characters also need to go through an arc so we can see how they grow and change throughout the film. Do they learn something? Do they have a new outlook on life? In *Harry Potter and the Sorcerer's Stone,* the protagonist learns to become a wizard. In *The Karate Kid* he learns how to defend himself. In *Lethal Weapon,* he starts out as a suicidal cop and recommits to life. In *Die Hard,* he heals his relationship with his estranged wife. In *Tootsie,* he goes from self-centered womanizer to understanding what women go through every day. And in *Casablanca,* he turns from a bitter, uncaring man into a virtuous patriot willing to sacrifice the love of his life for the betterment of mankind. In rare cases when the main character doesn't change, he almost always changes the lives of those around him.

THE PROTAGONIST

The most important character, of course, is your protagonist. In order to have a successful hero you must be aware of a few things:

1) **He must be active and drive the conflict.** He can be reactive at first, but then must take charge. Think about *The Fugitive.* Richard Kimble (Harrison Ford) is on his way to prison after being falsely convicted of killing his wife. Then a freak bus accident sets him free. He's on the run. For the next forty minutes, he runs, runs, runs to keep from being captured by a federal agent (Tommy Lee Jones). But then he gets active. He sets out to find the real killer and clear his name before he gets caught. This drives the movie. And remember, it is up to your protagonist to come up with the plans, get through the obstacles, and resolve his goal on his own. No cavalry can come in to save him.

2) **He must have a strong goal and will not compromise.** The goal is your Act 1 break. It's what the movie is about. It needs to be a strong goal—whether it be boy wants girl, cop hunts

killer, ship survives storm, etc.—and the hero will not stop until he achieves it. If the goal is a weak one, the movie will be too.

3) **He must face a series of ever-increasing obstacles but keep hope of achieving his goal.** Conflict and high stakes drive the film. The harder things get for your protagonist, the more engrossed the audience will be in the film.

4) **He must be special or unique in a meaningful way.** That doesn't mean he has to be a superhero. But he has to be someone whose journey we want to follow. Maybe he's funny, or kind, or romantic, or smart, or daring, or heroic. People go to the movies to escape reality and see bigger than life characters. Make sure yours is one of them.

5) **The audience must root for him and empathize.** We're going to follow his journey for ninety minutes. If we don't want him to succeed once his goal (Act 1 break) has been established, then it's going to be a very long ninety minutes. We need to feel for him, understand what he's going through, and hope he can somehow pull it off. When he does, we will leave the theater satisfied.

THE ANTAGONIST

What about your antagonist? His character is the mirror image of the protagonist.

1) **He may drive the conflict initially, but become reactive and be fighting for his life by the third act.** The antagonist's high point is the end of Act 2. His low point is the climax of the movie.

2) **He also has a strong goal and will not compromise.** And the better the antagonist, the higher the stakes, the more enjoyable the movie. Think about this: Which is a more exciting football game? When your favorite team wins 42–0? Or when your favorite team wins 42–41 on a last-second Hail Mary pass? They're both wins, but the latter will be a game you'll remember for a long time. Your movie should be that way too. Batman doesn't hunt down shoplifters; he goes after guys who want to rule the world.

3) **He faces obstacles as well, and through the second act, it looks like he is going to succeed.** He hangs in there for two acts, battling the protagonist and doing quite well. But then things fall apart for him in Act 3.

4) **He also must be unique.** Whether Darth Vader, an ex-boyfriend, a serial killer, a meteor heading to destroy Earth, or a drinking problem, "he" must be special.

5) **The audience must root against him and hope he fails.** If we're rooting for him to succeed, then your movie has some serious problems.

The names of your characters can also be telling. Sure, most of them are going to be typical names such as Pete or

Betty or Al or Rita. But certain names conjure up certain images. Crocodile Dundee, Indiana Jones, Rocky Balboa, and Luke Skywalker put a different image in our heads than do Homer Simpson, Pee-wee Herman, Ferris Bueller, or Willy Wonka. And don't forget about secondary characters. They need an identity all their own, but must never overshadow your protagonist.

RUNNING DIALOGUE

I once worked with a director who had clear instructions as to the kind of dialogue he wanted for his leading lady, known more for her beauty than her acting abilities. "No more than two syllable words," were the orders. Naturally, this limited the possibilities for scintillating conversation in my script. No matter. She was eventually replaced on the film (as was I), and the movie went straight to video, fading away into bisyllabic oblivion.

Good dialogue creates unique characters, propels the action forward, conveys pertinent information, and above all, engages us. "Go ahead, make my day." "May the Force be with you." "Frankly, my dear, I don't give a damn." "Show me the money!" All great lines (hmm, and bisyllabic as well) from classic films, something all writers strive for when putting words in our characters' mouths. But it is equally important to understand that in many instances, dialogue is *not* the best way to communicate action, message, or emotion. Truth is, it can be the worst. Movies are called motion pictures. And there's that old adage: a picture is worth a thousand words. What an audience sees can often communicate far more powerfully than any dialogue. Remember, a movie screen may be twenty feet high and fifty feet wide. A kiss, a teardrop, a wink, a sigh, a fist slamming on a table can be much more effective than anything a character could ever say. Therefore, find a way to use visuals first to tell your story before resorting to speech.

When you do use dialogue, it should be authentic, distinct, convincing, lively, and metaphorical. Ask yourself, "Is it natural? Do the characters all sound different? Am I using subtext?" This is when what the character says and what he means may be two entirely different things. Vito Corleone in *The Godfather* says, "I'm gonna make him an offer he can't refuse." That's a lot more subtle and clever than saying, "If he doesn't do what I want, I'll blow his freakin' brains out."

You also must be aware of "diction," which is defined as the choice and use of words. And the words you choose to have your characters say are determined by their education, profession, geographic location, and emotional states—all things I spoke about in the previous lesson. Look at the following two lines of dialogue. Both are spoken by a woman in a restaurant with her young son:

A) "Tommy, quit slouchin' in your seat and stop playin' with that dang salt shaker. I ain't gonna say it again.

One more time and you can kiss your dessert good-bye. Hear me?"

B) "Thomas, please, sit upright and leave the salt shaker alone. I'm not going to tell you again. Once more and there'll be no dessert for you, young man. Understood?"

Same situation, same message, but what can you tell about the mothers just from their diction? Mother #2 is in all likelihood better educated and more refined. The words we choose to use tell us a lot about the characters we create. For instance, how many different ways can a person say "hello," "get lost," or "that's great"?

HELLO	GET LOST	THAT'S GREAT
Hi	Beat it	Awesome
Howdy	Scram	Cool
Good morning	Take a hike	Super
What's up?	Leave	Sweet
Yo	Go	Wonderful

A young rapper will choose different words than a retired surgeon. Sometimes words are unique to a specific character. In *Casablanca,* when Victor, the freedom-fighting husband of Ilsa (Ingrid Bergman), wanted to show affection for her, he said, "I love you very much, my dear." When Rick (Humphrey Bogart) wanted to show affection for her, he said, "Here's looking at you, kid."

Here are a few other tips about dialogue:

1) **Dialogue has to be unique for each character.** No two people talk alike, even if they are twins. Mix it up and give them distinct personalities. This way, they'll react differently to whatever predicament you toss at them.

2) **People don't talk in full sentences.** Don't worry about proper grammar. Nobody speaks the way they write. Some lines of dialogue may be one word. Others may have no verbs or nouns. Listen to how people talk in everyday conversations and mimic that.

3) **Don't have your characters tell the audience things they will find out later.** This will only spoil the surprise. If your characters are planning a jewel heist, they shouldn't reveal the scheme beforehand, unless the plan is going to go awry.

4) **Avoid using clichés.** Be unique and original. Make your dialogue pop off the page. No "See you later, alligator." Come up with your own take on common expressions.

5) **Use dialogue to establish character relationships.** Find a way to introduce people in a clever manner. For instance, a woman storms up to a man at a cocktail party and says, "You were late picking up Timmy last night. Don't let it happen again!" This tells us they are probably a divorced couple, not on best of terms, who share custody of their child.

6) **Don't be too on the nose.** A woman paces about impatiently, glancing at her phone. Finally it rings. She answers it and says, "Yes, I'm happy you called. I've been waiting all day." Using subtext, she might actually say, "No, doing nothing, just hanging out." We know she's been waiting all day.

7) **Avoid mentioning things the movie audience will be able to see that the reader of the script cannot.** For instance, if two people are looking at a painting, your character might simply say, "It's beautiful," even though you might be tempted to say, "This painting is beautiful," because the reader cannot experience what the audience will see hanging on the wall.

8) **Don't be contradictory.** If a character says she hates the cold weather, don't have her go skiing later in the film without commenting on how cold it is.

9) **The last line spoken in a scene is the most important.** It contains the punch and has to have impact. Once it's been delivered, move on to the next scene.

10) **Don't start dialogue with words like "well," "you know," and "hey."** Yes, we all say those things every day, but it slows down a scene. Let the actors add those types of words when performing the lines if they so choose to.

11) **Eliminate words such as "hello" and "goodbye" when characters enter and exit scenes.** Start the scene later and end the scene earlier.

12) **Remember, your characters have history.** Most have met before the movie begins and would talk about things that

have occurred before then. You must work this into the script without leaving your audience in the dark.

13) **Don't be too reflective.** People don't talk to themselves. If you need to get out information, find a natural way to do it. Even in the movie *Cast Away,* Tom Hanks's character, alone on a tropical island, found a volleyball named Wilson to talk to. Save the long monologues for Shakespeare and the theater, where it is an acceptable means of communicating to the audience.

THE SUBPLOTS THICKEN

Every film has a main story (the "A" story) and one or more subplots (the "B" and "C" stories) which have their own beginnings, middles, and ends, and require their own setups, plot points, and resolutions. Subplots don't, however, follow the same timing in their structure as the "A" story and its major plot points.

Subplot characters are generally introduced in Act 1, but their stories and how they relate to the main story usually don't fully develop until Act 2. They crisscross the main plotline at pivotal moments, further engaging the audience in the narrative that is unfolding. Often, they involve the protagonist's best friend, romantic interest, a hobby, a family crisis, or some other event that the hero must deal with. For example, in *Trainwreck,* Amy Schumer's love life is the main plot. Her pending promotion and relationship with her co-workers is a subplot. In *Concussion,* Will Smith's discovery of brain disorders in NFL players is the main plot. His relationship with his wife and family is a subplot—as is Rocky's romance of Adrian, or the camaraderie between Randle McMurphy (Jack Nicholson) and his fellow mental patients in *One Flew Over the Cuckoo's Nest*.

There are several reasons why subplots are necessary:

1) **They offer the protagonist a chance to breathe.** If every scene were about the main story, the protagonist never has time to reflect on what has happened. The subplot helps with the pacing of the film and gives the hero, and the audience, opportunity to think about what will occur next. For instance, a cop chasing a killer may have to deal with his neglected wife. Or a man in love with a woman also spends time coaching a Little League team. Things like this allow us to see another side of our main character.

2) **They crisscross the main plotline at pivotal moments.** The subplot must be related in some way to the main plot. You can't have a romantic comedy and suddenly throw in an unrelated murder. However, you could have the best friend of the protagonist having relationship problems, and this helps your hero to work through his own personal issues.

3) **They express the story's theme.** Love conquers all. Greed is bad. Hard work will pay off. Reach for the moon and you'll get the stars. All storylines have to relate to a similar theme.

4) **They offer opportunities to witness changes in your protagonist.** A mean man who does something nice for a neighbor may get our sympathy and turn around how we feel about him. This is especially important if your protagonist isn't that likeable in the beginning.

The thing to remember is, subplot characters don't know they are part of a subplot, so you must write them as full and complex as your main characters, otherwise they simply become sounding boards for the protagonist.

FORMATTING LIKE A PRO

A while back, I spoke to a fellow screenwriting professor who told me that a student of his had turned in a script where every page had a different font. Perplexed, he asked her why she did this, and she answered, "I wanted my script to stand out." It stood out, all right. It made her look like a total amateur.

Before a writer starts writing a script, he needs to understand what a script is supposed to look like technically. Some people in the film industry maintain there is only one correct way to format a screenplay. However, by the multitude of styles found on the pages of many successful writers, one quickly realizes this can't be true. The fact is, there is no right or wrong way to format a script—just acceptable ways and unacceptable ways. An acceptable way makes you look like a professional, regardless of how well your characters, dialogue, and plot points stand up. An unacceptable way makes you look like an oblivious novice and will give readers a negative opinion of your work before they ever get to page two. What I present to you now is one acceptable way to format a feature-length screenplay, discussing the various elements (Scene Heading, Action, Dialogue, Transitions, etc.) of a script. It is the way I like to format my material. Other professionals may format their scripts slightly differently. Use these rules as a guideline. Not all scripts are brilliant, but there's no reason they can't look it.

GENERAL FORMAT

1) **FONT:** Use 12-point Courier typeface—nothing else. It's what they've been using since the days of the manual typewriter, when Courier first became the standard. With Courier, each letter is the exact same size, whether it's a 't' or a 'w', so page counts are always accurate. This isn't true of other fonts, even though others, like the popular Times New Roman, may be easier on the eye to read.

2) **PAGE NUMBERS:** Up top, aligned with the right margin, followed by a period. No page numbers shown on title page. Page numbering should be done automatically by your software so you shouldn't have to worry about this.

3) **SCRIPT LENGTH:** As previous stated, between 100 and 120 pages. Don't worry about rough drafts—they may be

significantly shorter or longer. You'll adjust that in the rewrites before you submit it to anyone.

4) **TITLE PAGE:** Title centered slightly above the middle of the page. The title of the script should be underlined and in CAPS. Below that the word "by." Below that the writer's name:

BUY MY SCRIPT

by

Larry Scribe

About 1.5 inches up from the bottom of the page, even with the left margin, put Registered WGA but don't include the registration number. On the same line, ending at the right margin, put your phone number. Under that put your email address. Don't put your home address. Some people think if you don't live in Los Angeles or New York, you can't be a serious writer. Don't put draft numbers. If it reads: 3rd draft, people will think the script is old and has been around. You want everyone to think they are reading a script hot off the press. Don't put dates. Someone may not read the script for weeks after you submit it. Again, you don't want anyone thinking it's old material.

5) PAPER: If you're sending a hard copy, it should be printed on 20 pound weight, 8.5" × 11", standard 3-hole punch multipurpose white paper. Only print on one side of a page. Fortunately, most people nowadays request a script be sent to them electronically as a PDF. This not only saves paper, which is good for the environment, but it saves you lots of money and time. A script can cost $5 minimum to copy and another $7 to mail out. Plus, with a hard copy, you have to write a cover letter, stick everything in an envelope, and take it to the post office. It only takes seconds to send someone a script as an attachment to an email.

6) SCRIPT COVER: Plain pastel-colored card stock paper. No words or graphics on the cover. Bind your scripts with 1.25" brass brads, top and bottom holes only. Again, this would only apply if sending out a hard copy.

7) PAGE MARGINS: Top 1", Bottom 1", Left Margin 1.5", Right Margin 1". The left margin has to be larger to account for the binding on a hard copy. Should your script be purchased and go into development, people will be getting hard copies.

8) ELEMENT MARGINS: What follows is a sample page from a script. Most software will set the proper margins for you, and some allow you to make adjustments. They don't have to be exactly what I list, but they should be pretty close. All text that is flush left starts 1.5 inches from the edge of the paper.

EXT. LARGE DRUGSTORE — DAY [SCENE HEADING]

Ralph, still in his pajamas, rushes up to Valerie, a
store employee, stocking toothpaste in an aisle.

←————2.25"————→ RALPH [CHARACTER]
Val... Val...!

                    VALERIE
          Ralph, what's the matter?

                    RALPH
          We're millionaires!

                    VALERIE
←——1.75"——→ (skeptical) [PARENTHETICAL]
          Millionaires? Have you been dip-
          ping into your cooking sherry?

                    RALPH
              (shaking his head, excited)
          Remember my Uncle Stan? He died
          and left me an apartment building!
          I just got the call.

                    VALERIE
          Uncle Stan? The smelly old boozer?

                    RALPH
←——1.25"——→Baby, he may have drunk and he may←——1.5"——→
          have stunk, but he was also worth
          a fortune. And Val, as his heir, I
          am too. Pack your bags. We're off
          to the Big Apple!

                    VALERIE
          New York City?! [DIALOGUE]

                    RALPH
          The fashionable East Side! We own
          a luxury apartment house on Park
          Avenue.

←————————————4.5"————————————→CUT TO: [TRANSITION]

9) FIRST PAGE: Scripts begin with the words FADE IN: though this is more tradition than anything else. This is followed by the first Scene Heading of your script:

```
FADE IN:

INT. SCIENCE LAB — DAY
```

Remember, you only have one chance to make a good first impression. The first ten pages of a spec script are critical. It's where the reader first forms his or her opinions about the writer, the story, the professionalism of the script, etc. Some things to consider:

A) Open with a great visual or situation to grab the reader's attention.

B) If you can, open on physical action.

C) Be sure you establish the genre or the film.

D) Make the dialogue unusually sharp.

E) Introduce your protagonist in a memorable manner.

10) TO EMPHASIZE A WORD: Underline it. Don't use bold or italics in your script. Bold stands out too much and italics are often missed on short words.

11) MORES & CONT'S: Don't use CONTINUED on the top and bottom of every page. Though older scripts used this, they are now only used in shooting scripts for production purposes. You may have to adjust your software to eliminate these.

12) TYPOS: Run spellcheck and proofread for grammatical errors.

SCENE HEADINGS

1) Scene headings are always in CAPS and begin with the abbreviations INT. or EXT. (for interior or exterior), followed by the location of the scene and the time it takes place:

```
INT. TOM'S HOUSE — DAY
```

2) Times of day should generally be limited to DAY and NIGHT, but in some instances, for clarity, MORNING, EVENING, LATER, or other similar words may be used.

3) To identify a specific location in a larger location, the specific location can be included in the Scene Heading:

```
INT. TOM'S HOUSE — KITCHEN — DAY
```

4) Whenever continuous action moves from inside to outside (or vice versa), a new Scene Heading is required as it would involve a new camera setup for shooting. If the action is immediate, the word SAME or CONTINUOUS replaces the time of day:

```
INT. TOM'S HOUSE — KITCHEN — DAY

Tom grabs his keys off the counter and races out
the back door.
```

EXT. TOM'S HOUSE — SAME

Tom rushes to his car, hops in, and roars off.

5) Be consistent with your Scene Headings. If the setting is TOM'S HOUSE in one scene, don't simply call it HOUSE or TOM'S PLACE in another scene. The Assistant Director needs to list all the locations when he breaks down the script. You don't want to confuse him.

6) Don't number your scenes. This in only done in a shooting script for production purposes.

SLUG LINES (OR SHOTS)

1) Slug Lines differ from Scene Headings in that they don't establish a new location. They call attention to what is important, or what the audience is seeing in a particular scene. They are written in ALL CAPS, flush with the left margin, on their own line:

INT. FOOTBALL STADIUM — DAY

Thousands of screaming fans cheer on the Bears.

THE FIELD

The Bears break from huddle and line up at scrimmage.

COACH ANDERSON

Sweat pours down his anxious face.

THE SCOREBOARD

Sixteen seconds left and counting, Bears down by four.

THE STANDS

Karen and Steve watch nervously.

BACK TO FIELD

Johnson snaps the ball and fades back to pass.

The Scene Heading location (Football Stadium) for all of the above Slug Lines is the same, but the focus of what we are seeing changes.

2) Slug Lines are also used when a character moves about within the same location:

INT. TOM'S HOUSE — KITCHEN — DAY

Tom grabs his keys off the counter and races into the

LIVING ROOM

He snatches his jacket off a chair and darts out the front door.

ACTION

1) Be visual but economical. Don't play art director.

INT. MOTEL ROOM — DAY

Small room with two double beds, faded bedspreads, flat-screen TV, three framed pictures of mountains

permanently fixed to the walls and several lamps,
one of which doesn't work.

This is bad. We all know what motel rooms have in them. Unless something you mention is germane to the script, it is unnecessary. This is better:

INT. MOTEL ROOM — DAY

Old, small and discount.

2) Use Action Verbs—Simple present tense is better than present progressive.

This is okay (passive):

A) Frank is walking briskly to his car.

B) Cindy is wearing a halter-top and a pair of tight jeans.

C) Howard is lying in the sun trying to get a tan.

D) Pam is running for the exit.

E) Mark is looking at the dog.

But this is better (active):

A) Franks dashes to his Audi.

B) Cindy sports a designer halter-top and snug jeans.

C) Howard sunbathes to a golden brown.

D) Pam scrambles for the exit.

E) Mark stares at the poodle.

3) Keep the narrative blocks to no more than five lines per paragraph. There should be plenty of "white" on the page.

4) Write in short, simple, tight sentences. Avoid lots of "and" or "as." This keeps things moving at a faster pace, especially during action scenes. Listing what we see makes for an easy read. For example:

```
EXT. WINDING ROAD — DAY

An empty two-lane road through a mountain pass.
A red FERRARI flies by.

Inside, GALLAGHER, rugged and buff, drives with a
desperate look on his face.

Behind him, a black PORSCHE pursues.

Gallagher checks his rear view mirror and sees the
Porsche gaining on him. He hits the gas.

FENWICK, intense with a scar on his cheek, franti-
cally drives the speeding Porsche. He pulls up
alongside Gallagher's vehicle and motions for him
to pull over.

Gallagher flips him "the finger" and continues on.
Fenwick slams his car into the Ferrari and sends it
barreling onto the grassy shoulder.

Gallagher struggles for control and manages to pull
back onto the road.

An oncoming CAR blares its horn.
```

```
Fenwick sees the oncoming car and steps on the gas.
He speeds up, heads directly toward the oncoming
car, then swerves out of the way in front of Galla-
gher's vehicle.

Fenwick slams on his brakes.

Gallagher smacks into the back of the Ferrari.
The two cars screech along the road attached by
their bumpers.

Fenwick turns his wheel and spins Gallagher's car
off the road and out of control.

It rolls several times and lands on its roof
```

5) Be specific rather than general:

   a. Sam puts the basket of fruit on the truck. (Okay)

   b. Sam heaves the basket of ripe peaches onto the Ford's flatbed. (Better)

6) Avoid using/repeating the same words . . . walks, looks, comes, goes, gets, enters, etc. You could say "get" for everything if you're not careful. "He gets up, gets breakfast, gets on the bus, gets to school, etc."

7) Don't cheat by telling the reader something that cannot be filmed.

   a. Lisa thinks about her poor test score and wonders if she'll ever get into college. (How will the audience know this, unless you did a voiceover?)

   b. Lisa glances at the "F" on her test sheet and starts to cry. (This we understand.)

8) Avoid describing routine action.

    a. Bob walks into the bathroom. He grabs his tooth-brush out of the medicine cabinet. He turns on the water, wets the brush, and smears toothpaste onto the bristles. (Unless this is germane to the scene, this is unnecessary.)

    b. Bob enters the bathroom and brushes his teeth. (Better)

9) Let the director direct. Avoid using camera angles, unless it is important to the story. For instance, if I wanted to show someone pouring poison into a glass, but didn't want the audience to know who that person was, I might say: "CLOSE-UP of HANDS pouring iodine into a glass." Otherwise, direct the reader's eye with your words.

    a. ANGLE ON: A motorcycle. (Bad)

    b. Steve creeps toward the motorcycle. (Better)

10) Avoid writing "starts to" and "begins to."

    c. Hank starts to mow the lawn. (Bad)

    d. Hank mows the lawn. (Better)

11) Don't pick out specific music for your script. 1) The director may hate the song you chose. 2) It may not be available. 3) It may cost too much to use. It's fine to generalize by saying: "'Friends in Low Places' by Garth Brooks plays on the jukebox" to establish you're at a country bar, as long as you understand a different song will probably be used.

12) Avoid repeating the Scene Heading descriptions in the narrative.

```
INT. BURGER KING — DAY

Kay scampers into Burger King. (Bad)


INT. BURGER KING — DAY

Kay scampers in. (Better)
```

13) Use the proper words . . .
   a. "its," "your," "their," and "whose" are possessive.
   b. "it's," "you're," "they're," and "who's" are contractions.
14) A character's name is written in ALL CAPS in the action element of the script only the first time he or she is introduced. After that, all characters are written in Title Case, including small parts like Taxi Driver.
15) To avoid confusing the reader, don't give characters names which begin with the same letter . . . e.g., John, Jane, Jessica, and Jack. On-screen, the audience will recognize who's who by their face. In the script, it's hard to keep track.
16) Keep character introductions brief. Don't cheat. For example:

```
MR. WILSON, 42, average height, honest as a day is
long, tender compassionate side, used to be a Boy
Scout, takes care of his mother . . . (Bad)
```

```
MR. WILSON, 40s, handsome, dedicated college
professor . . . (Better)
```

Remember, you never know what actor will want to play the part. Don't eliminate anyone by describing your character as being too specific an age or appearance, and above all, avoid using words like old, ugly, fat, or balding unless necessary for the part. What egotistical A-list actor sees himself as any of that?

CHARACTER

1) Don't center the character names in the script. Each name should start on the same left hand column of the page. Your software should do this for you, but if you center the character's name, it will not have a flush left margin.

2) If a character name changes, remind the reader what the character was initially called by placing it in parentheses after the new name the first time it changes:

```
          EDDIE (BUS DRIVER)
     Yeah, I met her in St. Louis
     last summer.
```

From here on the Bus Driver would only be called EDDIE.

3) Speech from a character that we do not see should have (O.S.), offscreen, or (V.O.), voiceover, after their

name. Offscreen is when the character is in the scene but not visible.

```
            HENRY (O.S.)
     It's me! I'm locked out!
```

Voiceover is used when a character is narrating the scene or we are hearing his thoughts.

```
            HENRY (V.O.)
     I'll never forget my old house
     in Whisper Falls . . .
```

4) If two characters speak the same thing at the same time, both their names go in the character cue, separated by a slash:

```
            BOB/CAROL
     You're kidding?!
```

DIALOGUE

1) It's best not to break dialogue in midsentence at the bottom of a page. But if you have to break up a passage due to length, use the word (MORE) after the speech at the bottom of the first page, and insert the word (CONT.) after the character name on the top of the next page.

```
            WILLIAM
     Sure, I remember Gloria. She
     used to live up the block
     from me.
            (MORE)
```

The next page would begin with:

```
              WILLIAM (CONT.)
         Great girl. Whatever happened
         to her?
```

Again, your software should do this for you.

2) Spell out numbers of ten or fewer in dialogue.

3) If the character is reading something out loud, the text being read should be in quotes under a parenthetical:

```
              BETTY
         I've got the address right here.
              (reading)
         "47 Sycamore Drive."
```

4) When using two columns of dialogue next to each other to show different simultaneous speeches, the left column should be slightly indented from the left margin.

```
    HARVEY                  MEGAN
We'd love to go.     Sorry, we're busy.
```

5) To show dialogue being spoken in a foreign language, write the lines in English underneath a parenthetical indicating the language:

```
              OLIVIA
         (in French, w/subtitles)
         A pleasure to meet you too,
         Mr. Silver.
```

Don't try to translate yourself. The reader may not know the language, or worse, may know it a lot better than you do.

6) There are several rules for phone conversations. If we only hear one side of the conversation, it should be written as follows:

```
                    STAN
          Frank, it's Stan, where are
          you?... That really sucks....
          Fine, I'll meet you at the
          club.
```

Use the ellipses to indicate a pause for listening time.

7) If we hear the other side of the phone conversation but don't see the person, it should be written this way, with a voiceover for the speaker we don't see:

```
                    STAN
          Frank, it's Stan, where are
          you?

                    FRANK (V.O.)
          Still at the office. My boss
          gave me a last minute assign-
          ment.

                    STAN
          That really sucks.

                    FRANK (V.O.)
          I'll be out of here in an hour.

                    STAN
          Fine, I'll meet you at the
          club.
```

8) If we see both people in the phone conversation, use both scene headings and the word INTERCUT to show we're going back and forth. The director will determine which person the camera is on at what point in the conversation during the editing of the movie.

INT. HEALTH CLUB — DAY

Stan sits in the locker room, talking on his cell phone.

          STAN
     Frank, it's Stan, where are
     you?

INT. FRANK'S OFFICE — SAME

Frank sits behind his desk, a pile of papers before him. He talks to Stan on his cell phone. INTERCUT.

          FRANK
     Still at the office.

          STAN
     You're kidding? How come?

          FRANK
     My boss gave me a last minute
     assignment.

          STAN
     That really sucks.

          FRANK
     I'll be out of here in an hour.

          STAN
     Fine, I'll meet you at the
     club.

He hangs up.

PARENTHETICAL

1) Parentheticals go on a line all to themselves, under the Character Cue and above the Dialogue, written entirely in lowercase letters.

2) They should start approximately five spaces to the right of where the dialogue begins.

3) If they wrap, the text should not wrap under the Parenthetical:

```
                    TYLER
          (barely able to speak
          coherently)
      But you said she was doing
      better.
```

4) Parenthetical directions are only used to describe the way the character delivers the line. They are not used to describe action and are not written in complete sentences. Sometimes, however, writers cheat. You might put simple actions in a parenthetical, such as (sitting down), (lighting a cigarette), (opening a window). It makes the script read faster.

5) If the Parenthetical breaks up a segment of dialogue, the dialogue should begin and end in an ellipsis:

```
                    MARIA
      I wanted to come see you,
      but...
            (beat)
      ...frankly, you scare me.
```

TRANSITIONS

1) Transitions appear on the right side of the page, in ALL CAPS, followed by a colon. Only FADE IN: appears flush left.

2) CUT TO: is used when a scene changes time and location. You can change scene headings without using a transition.

3) DISSOLVE TO: is used to blend one scene into another.

4) FADE OUT: is used when the screen goes black.

5) Some writers use no transitions in their scripts. Instead, they might triple space between change of scene headings (as opposed to double space).

FLASHBACKS AND MONTAGES

1) Use Flashbacks sparingly. They tend to interrupt the flow of the action.

2) If the Flashback is just one scene, you can write (FLASHBACK) in the scene heading:

INT. BOOKSTORE — DAY (FLASHBACK)

3) Longer Flashbacks that involve more than one scene are indicated by inserting the slug line BEGIN FLASHBACK above a scene heading:

BEGIN FLASHBACK

INT. AIRPORT TERMINAL — DAY

```
Molly grabs her bags off the luggage carousel and
heads for the exit.
```

When the Flashback is over, the following slug line is inserted at the end, flush left:

```
END FLASHBACK
```

A montage or series of shots is used to show a progression of action that occurs over time in a quick, economical manner on-screen. For example, if a couple has just met and we want to show the growth of their relationship without taking up a lot of screen time, we would use a montage:

```
QUICK SHOTS of Larry and Beth getting to know each
other better over the next several days. Among what
we see are:

     a) Larry and Beth eat dinner together.
     b) The two cheer the Dodgers at a baseball game.
     c) Beth introduces Larry to her mother.
     d) The two hold hands while strolling in the park.
     e) Larry and Beth kiss under the bridge at sunset.
```

In the actual movie, there may be a dozen scenes showing the growth of their relationship, and none of the ones you came up with may be included. But it gives the reader and director an idea of the *type* of scenes we'll be seeing on-screen without taking up a lot of pages.

In conclusion, follow the basic rules of formatting, but find a style that you're comfortable with. Even your first script should make you look like a pro.

PART TWO

THE BUSINESS SIDE OF SCREENWRITING

WHAT IT TAKES TO BECOME A SUCCESS

I didn't always want to be a professional writer. With a degree in biology from the University of Pennsylvania, and courses such as Organic Chemistry, Molecular Genetics, and Astrophysics under my belt, I initially pursued an entirely different career path—stand-up comedy, the only logical choice based on the grades I received in those classes. But after hitting the New York comedy clubs for a year, and dodging my fair share of martini olives and maraschino cherries, I realized *writing* comedy and not performing it offered a much more promising (and healthier) future. An ardent movie fan, I naively fled to Los Angeles to foolishly pursue my dreams of writing screenplays.

Back then, we were all watching MTV videos, buying 40-megabyte-hard-drive computers, and flourishing (or suffering) on a big dose of Reaganomics. For the aspiring screenwriter, there was limited information available on how to begin a filmwriting career. The internet hadn't been invented, very few "how to" books graced the bookstore shelves, and film schools were not yet popular. Personally, I had no idea what a movie script even looked like, and my knowledge of the business side of Hollywood was beyond pathetic. I thought you simply wrote a script, mailed it in to the Warner Bros. story department, and a few weeks later they sent you a check. Sometimes being stupid is a blessing.

Had I known that the odds of actually selling my work and establishing a lucrative career were miniscule, I might never have bought that old Ford Econoline van for $300, piled all my belongings into it, and driven three thousand miles to the West Coast in search of fame and fortune. To support myself in those early years, I scooped ice cream at a drugstore . . . installed telephones for the phone company . . . peddled beer at a baseball stadium . . . sold luggage at a department store . . . collected specimens for a medical lab (don't ask) . . . and the ultimate pièce de résistance jobapalooza, worked at a pharmaceutical testing facility where I ran the hemorrhoid cream study, picking up four hundred rats three times a day and smearing their little bottoms with some newfangled Preparation H. There was no job too demeaning for *this* Ivy League graduate. I know my mother was proud.

Sadly, none of these character-building experiences helped jumpstart my career, though I did get to ride in a hospital elevator one day with a three-hundred-pound Orson Welles, who glared at me with such enmity, I could barely manage to mutter the word, "Rosebud . . ." Fortunately, I did find a couple of classes to take on the subject of screenwriting. The first was at UCLA Extension. It was taught by a successful scriptwriter who had had several of his screenplays produced. The class consisted primarily of this writer telling everyone his experiences in Hollywood—the famous actors he knew (good friends with Jack Nicholson), the cool parties he went to, the fancy cars he drove. While vastly entertaining, it provided little benefit to the novice writer on how to construct a script, get it out to buyers, and advance a career.

The other class I took was at Santa Monica Junior College, taught by an old-time network TV writer. Here, we worked on an original script and read scenes aloud to the class every week. Most of the class was comprised of hopeful middle-aged English-teacher types who truly believed that one day a golden Oscar would be perched on their fireplace mantel. Unfortunately, the pages they read were mostly dismal and their subject matter even worse. One fellow wrote a script about farm machinery because "we've never seen a movie about farm machinery before." It went something like this:

```
          JOHN
     Mary, did you see the keys to
     the tractor?

          MARY
     No, John, where did you leave
     them?

          JOHN
     I thought, in the kitchen.

          MARY
     Well you better find them.
     The corn is getting quite long.
```

There's a reason we've never seen a movie about farm machinery.

My script, however, was a comedy and my fellow students laughed heartily when I read my pages out loud. I knew I was on to something, though I was still a few years away from making my first sale. This class, while encouraging, did not further my career. However, it did provide one very important pearl of wisdom that I reiterate today to all my students on the first day of every semester. I tell them, "It takes four things to become a successful screenwriter." They are:

1) **TALENT:** You've got it or you don't. The Man (or Woman) upstairs gave us the ability to be better than others at certain things, and nothing you can do will increase or decrease the gifts you were born with. Jordan Spieth, Serena Williams, and Steph Curry are talented athletes. John Legend, Bruno Mars, and Katy Perry are talented musicians. Others may be talented writers, perhaps you. But talent alone does not equal success. You still need the three other elements to make it in the film business.

2) **CRAFT:** Learning how to write a good script is the next most important aspect of becoming a successful screenwriter. And the good thing is, anyone can be taught. How is a professional script formatted? What does real dialogue sound like? How can you create

intriguing characters? What's the structure of a feature film? You can't play tennis if you don't know how to serve the ball. You can't play the piano if you don't understand chords and harmonies. Similarly, you can't write a good script if you don't know the basics of writing. But any class (and hopefully this book) can teach this to you.

Unfortunately, even talent and a well-written script will only get you so far. There are thousands of brilliant writers with wonderful scripts living throughout the country right now. And no one will ever know about them. Why? Because they lack the third element of success.

3) **OPPORTUNITY:** If no one ever reads your script, no one will ever discover how good it is, or how good a writer you are. You need to create opportunities for your work to be seen, and this means contacting and meeting lots of people. You never know which one might one day be helpful to you. You may have to contact a hundred agents or managers, tell them the premise of your script, and hope that a couple of them are willing to read it. You may have to move to Los Angeles where you can work or intern at an entertainment company and make valuable connections. (Skip handing out your script to strangers at busy intersections—it's been done.)

Other ways to meet people and create opportunities are to take an acting class, go to as many social events as possible, join a gym and befriend everyone. I knew a writer who made great industry connections selling drugs, though that does come with certain consequences. Just remember, in LA, nearly everyone you meet is working, wants to work, or used to work in the entertainment business. Ninety-nine percent will never become successful. But should you stay friends with the one who does, you may have a career that others only fantasize about.

I will discuss creating opportunities in more detail later in this book. But even a talented writer with a great script that everyone wants to read will still need the final element in order to become successful.

4) **LUCK:** As the saying goes, timing is everything. Big A-list actor tells his agent he wants to do a romantic comedy that will send him to Paris for two months. Your script happens to land on that agent's desk that morning . . . and is a romantic comedy set in Paris. Bingo! Or big A-list producer's Porsche gets a flat tire on the freeway. You, chugging along in your beat-up Honda, see the stranded motorist and offer to help. When you realize who he is, you ask politely if he'll read your script. He reluctantly agrees and loves it. Luck cannot be planned. It just happens. And luck is as impor-

tant as talent, and opportunity is as important as craft.

Should all these elements come together, after a few long years, you may become an overnight success, or at least the "flavor of the month." This could translate to multiple deals, big money, even offices on a studio lot. I was given an office on the Paramount lot after my second deal. Upon arriving there my first day, I excitedly saw a nameplate on my door that read, ANDY ROSE. Then I turned to the office across the hall from me and read the nameplate on that door. It read, WILL FUKUTO. It wasn't long before I realized they will indeed.

MY SCRIPT IS FINISHED, NOW WHAT?

Congratulations! Your script is finished. You've rewritten it a half-dozen times. All your friends love it. You just know it's going to sell for millions. But before you submit it to anyone, ask yourself one simple question: Is it monumentally outstanding? For that's how good it needs to be to distinguish your work from that of thousands of other new writers who believe they're going to sell their new script for millions as well. If it's not, put it aside and start on another . . . and another . . . and another, until you're sure the answer to that one simple question is, "Absolutely!"

Understand, it's tough to make good contacts in the film business, and you don't want to waste any on a screenplay that's merely ordinary. Keep writing and you will continue to get better, just like the tennis player who hits a thousand balls, or the piano player who started with Chopsticks and now performs Rachmaninoff. Once you're absolutely certain you have something really special, your script is ready to go out into the marketplace. That's when the *real* work begins.

The hardest thing you will ever have to do to become a professional screenwriter (other than navigate the San Diego Freeway at rush hour) is breaking in to the business. The good news is, once you've established yourself as a working writer within the industry, you can have a long and prosperous career just by being mediocre. Okay, I'm not trying to say that most working writers are talentless hacks, but have you been to the movies lately? Would you consider the product you're seeing on-screen to be clever, ingenious, stimulating, witty, or intelligent? Sure, some of it is, and we should be thankful for the dozens of great films that come out every year. But someone also wrote *Sharknado 4* and got paid handsomely to do so. Now, I'm not suggesting you set your standards to the lowest common denominator. Hopefully, you can turn out the kind of material that is critically acclaimed, enjoyed by many, and makes a little money as well. But I am saying that you don't have to be a literary whiz to make it as a successful screenwriter.

Let's talk history for a minute. The movie business is about making money. It always has been. That's why they call it a business. Back in the 1930s, Adolph Zukor (Paramount), Darryl Zanuck (20th Century Fox), Harry Cohn (Columbia), and their powerful mogul cronies had to answer to the bankers in New York, just as the heads of Paramount (Viacom), 20th Century Fox (Newscorp), and Columbia (Sony) have to answer to their stockholders today. The thing is, today the stakes are much higher. In the 1930s, the cost of an average picture was a mere $1 million. Granted, we have to account for inflation, and there were not nearly as many ancillary outlets then as there are today. The foreign market was small, there were no DVDs or streaming, cable didn't exist (come to think of it, TV didn't exist), and the price of a ticket was under a buck.

But today, the average cost of a studio movie is closing in on $100 million, twice that if the film has extensive computer graphics. Then throw in another $50 million to market it, and you can see why one bomb can have devastating effects on a company. That's why Hollywood does not like to take chances on the unknown, which is YOU, an unsold writer with an original screenplay. Instead, studio production slates nowadays are filled with sequels, remakes, movie versions of old TV shows, bestselling books, adventures of comic book superheroes, and pet projects of big stars and directors. Anything that has built-in marketing to attract an initial audience has one step up on the competition. This is great if you're an established writer looking for his next high-paying assignment. It's not so great if you're a young writer looking to sell his first spec script.

So how do you break in? The easiest way is to call your old friend Leonardo or your distant cousin Scarlett and see if they'll make a few phone calls for you. Referrals (which I'll talk about more in a later lesson) mean everything in the movie business and almost always guarantee you a return phone call and at least some token consideration. After all, an agent, manager, or producer ignoring a favor asked of him by a powerful box office star is akin to committing hara-kiri in this business. Of course, it doesn't have to be someone on the A-list who makes a call for you. Anyone who knows anyone can be extremely helpful and get people to take you seriously . . . well, at least give you a shot.

Unfortunately, most young writers do not know anyone in the movie business, other than the kid who takes their ticket stub at the downtown multiplex. Therefore, you're going to have to work a bit harder to break in. It's not impossible. Just make sure you have thick skin.

BUILD A CONTACT LIST

Since you don't know anyone in the business, you need to make yourself a list of people you can approach to see if they will read your script. This list will include agents, managers, and producers. (I will explain the differences among these roles, along with those of lawyers and executives, in the next two chapters.) Among the most popular resources are the subscription services StudioSystem and IMDb Pro (which sometimes offers a free one-month trial), and *Hollywood Screenwriting Directory* (available for purchase online, and updated several times a year). These sources contain listings of specific agents, managers, and producers, usually with addresses, email addresses, and phone numbers. Contacting people cold is easy. Getting them to respond back is what's tough. Most of the bigger firms state that they do not accept unsolicited material, so there's really no point in contacting those places cold. Some of the smaller companies are more likely to be interested in new talent, and that is from where you should make your list. You're going to face a lot of rejection, but remember, you don't need fifty people to read and like your script. You only need one to jumpstart your career.

WRITE A GREAT QUERY MESSAGE

Once you've made your list, it's time to send out a query message to see if the person you're contacting would be willing to read your script. Unfortunately, 95 percent of those you approach will never get back to you. Of those who do, most will send you a polite rejection message, telling you, "Your idea just isn't what's selling now . . . the movie business is subjective, so you may have better luck with another company . . . in a year we'll be kicking ourselves . . . blah blah blah." These standard responses may be addressed to you, or they may be made out to the person they sent it to earlier that day but carelessly forgot to change the name. I've gotten plenty of "Dear Bill" or "Dear George" salutations over the years.

You'll notice I talk about messages. This means email. In the old days (as in a mere twenty years ago), you might send a snail mail letter, but that is just not done in today's high-tech world. You could try calling a company on the phone, but the assistant who answers will most likely tell you they don't accept unsolicited scripts. Sure, she'll take a message and hand it to her boss, but the chance of getting a call back is about the same as winning the Powerball lottery. (And if you did that, screw the agents, managers, and producers—you can finance your own movie!)

What should you say in a query message? Let's start with what *not* to say. Don't make it seem like you are doing them a favor by allowing them to read your wonderful script. Don't be demanding, pompous, arrogant, overconfident, or play games. Don't go on endlessly by telling them about your extraordinary credentials and how your script is going to make them millions of dollars and win them an Academy Award. Here is an example of a DON'T send message:

Script Buyer
Gimme a Break Films
Dear Sir,

I'm writing you because I want to give you a once-in-a-lifetime opportunity to buy my new thriller screenplay, Too Sick to Die, guaranteed to be a huge blockbuster. It's about a man and woman who find love under the strangest of circumstances. A far better romance than Titanic, with more drama than Casablanca. Everyone who has read it thinks it's Oscar caliber and I'm sure you will too. I've attached the script as a PDF and will call you next week to talk deal. Enjoy! Oh, and by the way, I'd also like to direct.

Sincerely,
Johnny Oblivious

Okay, a bit of an exaggeration on my part, but you do see the problems here? Let's start with the heading. Know who you're sending your message to and address them personally, not with a basic "sir" or "ma'am" (or worse, "dude"). Then ask them if they would *consider* reading your screenplay. They're the ones doing you the favor. Follow that with a logline that actually describes your movie, not some generic blurb that could apply to fifty different films. Don't make ridiculous comparisons to other movies. It's fine to compare it in tone to others, such as "a Judd Apatow type comedy," but leave it at that. And don't be presumptuous and attach your script unless they ask to read it. If they do, it will probably take weeks for them to get back to you, so don't pester them with calls or messages. A polite follow-up message a month later is fine, but that's still not going to increase the odds of ever hearing from them. And above all, forget about directing, starring in, producing, or catering the movie. Right now, you just want them to read the darn script. Make your initial message succinct but informative enough to pique their interest in your work and in you.

Here is a DO send message:

Dear Mr. Storey,

I've recently completed a screenplay entitled "Too Sick to Die" and would like to submit it to your company for consideration. It is a thriller about a terminally ill man and woman who accidently discover a black market for organ transplants and must decide whether to reveal the scheme to authorities and risk their own lives, or look the other way and receive the treatments they need in order to survive. Along the way, their newly acquired knowledge puts them in grave danger, and only through their growing love can they stay strong and do the right thing.

Through my years of working at a hospital dialysis center, I've come to understand the frustrations of patients waiting for organs and the desperate things they will do to receive one. I've had an article published in my local paper on this subject, as well as a short story in a national magazine, which was well received. Thanks again for your time and I look forward to hearing from you soon.

Sincerely,
Kris Writer

This message is short, professional, and to the point. It states the logline, followed by the add-on. Then the writer talks about her background, her knowledge of the subject matter, and that she has been published before. If you're young and don't have much of a résumé yet, mention your education, why you're interested in film, and how much you enjoy some of the movies their company has made (if contacting a producer). Hopefully, all this would be enough to get someone to take a chance and ask to read the script.

And while we're on the subject of queries, I'm often asked how important a good title is to selling a script. The answer is, it can certainly help, as the name of the movie will ultimately become a key marketing tool. Films like *Psycho, Die Hard, Top Gun, Apocalypse Now,* and *Animal House* have clever titles that are easy to remember and describe their stories well. Conversely, how many of you remember the movies *We Bought a Zoo, V.I. Warshawski, The Men Who Stare at Goats, Operation Dumbo Drop,* or *Dude, Where's My Car?* Bottom line, if a buyer is interested in the material, he's not going to care what you're calling it right now. The financier and distributor will come up with something catchy down the line.

As a side note, be aware that you can't copyright a title and it's difficult to trademark one as well. The only way that can be done is if the movie is out and is so well known that it needs protection to distinguish it from others. Usually, that's because of potential business opportunities that can arise from that name. For instance, there has been more than one film made called *Bad Boys, Heaven Can Wait, The Kid, Crash,* and *Flawless.* None were distinct enough or marketable enough to warrant a trademark. But don't try calling your next script *Star Wars.* That name is so well known and identified with George Lucas's concept and characters that in that situation, a trademark applies.

Regardless of title, the reality of the business is, 95 percent of the people you contact cold with a query message will not get back to you. So you have to do other things to promote your career.

ENTER CONTESTS

There are dozens of screenplay contests that you can enter, some small, some more prestigious. A simple internet search will lead you to most of them. They all have one thing in common: It costs money to participate, usually in the $25 to $50 range. The question is, is this money well spent? In order to answer that, you have to know what you will get out of entering. Some contests are simply in it for the submission fee. They'll name a winner, some runners-up, some honorable mentions, pay out some prize money (anywhere from a few hundred to several thousand dollars), and that's it. Others go one step further, claiming to send loglines of the winning scripts to "established professionals" in the entertainment industry, and get you meetings with agents and producers. A few contests say they will give you brief feedback on your script, which is always valuable, though often you pay extra for this service. But none can really promise you anything. Sure, it's nice to win some cash and be acknowledged, but that in and of itself is not going to put a whole lot of groceries on the table for long. Sure, some contest winners have gone on to have productive careers in Hollywood. But it is a small percentage of those who enter.

However, if your script is recognized as one of the best, you can use this acclaim as a selling tool when contacting people in your query messages, particularly if it's one of the better-known contests. After all, if someone found merit with your script, then it must be good, right? The main thing is, research the contest before entering it. Do a hundred people submit scripts or seven thousand? Have any winners actually sold their work to the industry? Will you hear anything from these people if you're not one of the chosen few? There's no point in entering a contest if the only winners are the people collecting your entry fee.

Don't confuse contests with readers who charge to critique your work. Some of these people claim to have worked for a big-time producer at a big-time studio. Now they are willing to help you with your project—for a fee. They may read it and give you a page of notes for $100, three pages of notes and a half-hour phone consultation for $300, work with you on the script for $500, and even offer to rewrite it for you for $1,000. Beware of these arrangements. Many of these script consultants are much more interested in their own monetary success than in yours. Sure, they may have the knowledge to help you make your script saleable, but if they're that good, why aren't they still working for that big-time producer at that big-time studio? Better yet, why aren't they selling their own scripts? Instead, have your friends read your script and see what they think. Even if they're not writers, you'd be surprised at some of the good comments an intelligent novice can give you.

ATTEND EXPOS

Every year, some private entrepreneurs organize a mini-convention, or expo, at a large hotel, usually in New York or Los Angeles. They invite dozens of producers, agents, managers, and executives (all usually lower-level) to come sit on panels, conduct classes, answer questions, and discuss the entertainment industry with wannabe writers, actors, directors, and producers. It generally costs a few hundred dollars to attend these two- or three-day events, and if you know little about the movie business, it's a good way to get your feet wet. They can be interesting and informative. Whether they are worth spending the money on depends on your budget. The bottom line is, can attending an expo help your career? Maybe.

Some of these events also have a pitch session, though it may cost extra. It's kind of like the speed dating of loglines. You go from chair to chair and get three minutes to tell an industry professional your idea and hear their comments. Then you move on to the next person. In some cases, you may have a certain number of pitches that you have paid for, and you get to choose to whom you would like to pitch. Should one of these people take a liking to your story, they may give you their business card and offer to read the script. Stranger things have happened.

APPLY TO INDUSTRY WRITING PROGRAMS

Several production companies actually offer introductory paying jobs to fledgling writers, though usually designed more for the TV writer than the feature writer. Disney/ABC has a one-year program where writers meet with executives, producers, and agents and learn the business from the ground up. Pay is about a grand a week. HBO has an eight-month writing fellowship program where a "diverse" group of writers are mentored by creative executives and develop a script suitable for their channel. They pay a "small stipend." Warner Bros. has had a writers' workshop for more than thirty years. It consists of lectures and working on scripts in a group environment with the goal of getting a staff position on a show. They do not offer compensation. Other programs include the Academy Nicholl Fellowship in Screenwriting, as well as a salaried position with the Nickelodeon Writing Program. Check each of their websites for specific details about application requirement. Be aware, however, thousands of people apply for a limited number of positions, so competition is fierce. Most require you to submit a résumé, bio, writing samples, and letters of recommendation to apply.

SEEK INTERNSHIPS

Are you willing to work for free? Everyone loves to get something for nothing, and free labor is definitely something.

Many studios and companies have both formal and informal internship programs, particularly in the summer. You can apply and, if accepted, will work for a legitimate moviemaker. Some may even pay you a nominal salary. They're not specifically about writing, as the previously mentioned programs are. You'll be answering phones, typing letters, fetching coffee, copying scripts, and maybe even reading a few and critiquing them. It may not be as much fun as that counselor job you had at Camp Nincompoop the previous summer, but you are making contacts, and that is the name of the game in the entertainment business. If you are well liked, an internship can lead to a permanent job, or at the very least some good contacts to get your script read down the line.

BECOME AN AGENT TRAINEE

All of the big agencies (CAA, ICM, WME, UTA, etc.) have agent trainee programs, and many successful professionals have come out of them, including luminaries like David Geffen, Barry Diller, and Rich Ross. The usual requirements are that you be a college graduate, have an interest in learning the business, look professional, and be reasonably sane (at least by Hollywood standards). They're simple to apply to. Just call the main switchboard of the agency for details, or ask to speak to the person in charge of the program. Many allow you to submit an application online. If they are interested in you, they will contact you to come in for an interview. You'll have to pay your own way to LA, but the experience will be worth it. Wear your best business clothes and be prepared to show off your knowledge of the film business and enthusiastically explain why you want to work there. You don't necessarily have to want to become an agent (though don't tell them that). The truth is, most members of these trainee programs do not actually become agents, but they do move on to other careers in the entertainment business.

Now, before you get too excited, please note, it's very competitive. Only about 10 percent of all applicants get accepted. You will spend your first six months working long hours in the mailroom for minimum wage, something you may not have envisioned doing after graduating Harvard with a B.A. in English Lit. If you survive, you'll get promoted to an agent's desk where you'll answer phones and type letters for another six months for even longer hours. Hopefully, the person you're working for treats you with some compassion, because some agents use the trainees as their whipping boys/girls and make life miserable for them. After the year is up, the senior agents will determine if you are junior agent material, and you will determine how much longer you can stand this job. Should you decide to part ways, they will usually try to find you another position in the industry. But the good news is, even if they don't, you'll have made dozens of contacts with everyone in town and can probably find your own gig. Plus, when you finish that script you've been working on, you can send it to any one of the many agents you got to know while being a trainee. A lot of agents have become successful writers.

CONTACT ALUMNI

Did you graduate from college? It's a good bet that someone from your school is working in the entertainment business. See if your alumni relations office can help you track them down. Then contact them and see if they would be willing to chat with you for a few minutes, even just over the phone. Don't ask them for anything . . . yet. But if you can establish some rapport, maybe in an avuncular sort of way, they can refer you to someone who could be helpful to you. Better yet, you never know when a nostalgic soul with fond memories of trashy frat parties, ditching class, Ultimate Frisbee, and greasy football tailgate chow might even choose to mentor you.

MOVE TO LOS ANGELES

Not to harp on the obvious, but they ain't developing a lot of movies in Chippewa Falls. If you're young and don't have a family, a good job, or any real responsibilities (hmm, sounds like most recent college grads), go pack your bags and move to LA. Yes, it's a bold move. You may not know anyone out there, it's expensive, the traffic is horrendous, the crime rampant, the smog unbearable—but all in a good way. Besides, you need to make contacts and this is the place to do it. Everyone you meet out there knows someone in the business, and you never know who might be able to help you out some day. (The roommate of an ex-girlfriend's friend had a small struggling management company when I met him. Ten years later he was president of a major studio.) Find a roommate to cut costs, then socialize. Go to parties. Join a gym. Take classes. Get out and meet people. And give it a couple of years. That's the minimum amount of time it takes to become an overnight success. In the interim, you can enjoy those 70 degree January days, surfing in the morning and snow skiing in the afternoon. And the margaritas are to die for.

GO TO COLLEGE

There are not a lot of eighteen-year-olds out there who are ready to become professional screenwriters. You just haven't lived long enough to have gained ample worldly experiences to compete professionally, nor have you had sufficient time to hone your writing skills. My advice, therefore, is if you have the opportunity to go to college, do so. You'll learn something (even if it's just how to drink heavily and still make it to class in the morning) and figure out what you really want to do when you grow up.

My students ask me all the time about whether they should attend grad school. There are dozens of master's programs in film throughout the country. If you get into a prestigious one like USC, UCLA, NYU, or AFI, then go. You will not only get a great hands-on film education taught by industry professionals, but you will also gain access to the vast alumni networks these schools offer. And as I keep saying, who you know is as important as what you know. In fact, that's so important, I'll say it again. Who you know is as important as what you know.

But what about other less prominent schools? While other programs across the country can be valuable, you must consider whether the cost of the education will pay off in the long run. A year at a private college today can run $50,000 and up, and I've known just as many high school dropouts working in Hollywood as I have Ph.D.s. Back in those nostalgic '90s, a *junior* high school dropout was made co president of a major studio. So while knowledge is valuable, you need to ask yourself, is grad school just delaying the inevitable at a steep price? The truth is, nobody in the film business really cares about your formal education. If you have a good script, that's all anyone wants. As one high-ranking executive once told me, "We're whores at this studio; we'll work with anyone."

I do, however, recommend you take some individual classes, especially if you move to LA. Besides those screenwriting courses I mentioned, I also took an improvisational acting class, which introduced me to a number of people in the industry and even led to doing some postproduction looping (voiceover work) on one of the Indiana Jones films. I grunt really well when thrown off a truck.

OTHER THINGS YOU CAN DO

Since the name of the game is to make contacts, any job you can get that puts you in touch with people who can help your career is worth considering. I was once a production assistant on a low-budget film. My job included cleaning out a trash dumpster, running to the drugstore to get supplies for the makeup artist, and delivering script pages to some of the actors. Not exactly a prestigious gig, but I did make some contacts. Another job might be being a personal assistant to an actor, director, or producer. This generally involves non-industry-related tasks, such as picking up the kids at school or being at their home when the plumber arrives. But again, you will make contacts. If you have some individual skills, you might be a personal trainer, yoga instructor, or chef to people who could assist you in your writing career one day. I once knew a would-be writer who worked at a funeral parlor. Unfortunately, the contacts he made there were no longer able to help him.

MAKE A MOVIE

No, I don't mean some multi-million-dollar feature-length extravaganza. But a creative ten-minute short that you wrote, directed, and uploaded onto YouTube can become a calling card. It's easy to do, not very expensive to shoot video, and you can edit it on your home computer. If it's clever, original, and catchy, people will recognize that. Everyone has a script, but not everyone has footage. And people in the business today, particularly millennials, would much rather watch something than read something. If they like what they see, maybe then they'll ask to read your script.

AGENTS, MANAGERS, AND LAWYERS

Relationships. They are the essence of Hollywood, and I don't mean the ones you read about on *TMZ*. I'm talking about relationships with people who will make a difference in your career. Agents, managers, and lawyers. To be a successful screenwriter you need at least one, if not all three, to become a big part of your life. (I could add therapists but that would be a chapter unto itself.) Each of these representatives has a specific role—agents find you work, managers guide your career, lawyers negotiate your agreements—though there is much overlap in what they do.

AGENTS

The rep you need most is an agent. They are also the most difficult to get when you're first starting out. Most agents are looking for established writers because nurturing a new writer's career takes up a whole lot of time that could otherwise be spent on clients who already have industry connections and are easier to sell. Plus, established writers have established fees (called quotes) that an agent can build on and improve. A newbie is starting from scratch, and agents work on commission. The more money you make, the more they make, though sometimes the quest for that ultimate dollar can lead to overly aggressive negotiations. I once heard about a writer whose agent got him a job to do an adaptation of *A Tale of Two Cities*. As part of the contract, the agent demanded his client get novelization rights—the right to turn the screenplay into a book. The studio informed him they were quite happy with the Dickens version and the adamant agent almost blew the deal.

WHAT AGENTS DO

An agent's job is to sell screenplays, find you writing assignments, package projects, negotiate your deal, and give you basic feedback on your scripts. But there are a lot of other things they must do before any money rolls in, especially with a new writer. Agents make it their business to not only know about all the jobs that are out there as soon as they are available, but to build relationships with as many studio executives and producers as they can so that business also becomes personal. This way they get inside information on what types of projects people are really looking for, and what is actually selling. Agents also bring an added bonus: They have the best gossip in town. I remember hearing a juicy tidbit weeks before it became public about a studio president I had just met who was revealed to be a former porn star.

When an agent signs someone new, it's usually because he read a promising spec script and really liked it. That script now has to be sent to dozens of producers, follow-up calls have to be made, meetings must be set and reset, lunches need to be swallowed, then another round of follow-up calls. The hope is that at least one of these producers will want to attach themselves to the screenplay and take it in to a studio for a quick sale. But even if none are interested in being involved in that particular project, it still serves as an all-important writing sample. If a producer or executive likes your writing, they may be willing to hire you for an open assignment or even invite you in to pitch them an original idea of yours they just might pay you to write.

In California, agents are licensed and regulated to ensure financial responsibility. They cannot produce films with any clients and are not entitled to take more than a 10 percent commission. Agencies are also almost always franchised by the Writers Guild and agree to abide by various Guild-mandated rules in the agencies' contracts with writers. One of these WGA provisions states that an agency agreement cannot exceed two years and that if, during that two-year period, your agent doesn't find you work (at least a legitimate offer, even if you turn it down) during any ninety-day period, you can fire your agent and move on—unless, of course, you are currently working on something your agent got you. After all, it costs your agent nothing to keep you on his roster. It costs you your mortgage payments and a trip to Aruba if he is unproductive.

TYPES OF AGENCIES

Some agencies represent writers, directors, actors, and producers. They are called talent agencies. Some represent only writers and directors, and are called literary agencies. (Agencies that only represent actors are also called talent agencies.) There are large, midsize, and small or boutique agencies, all of whom do excellent, and sometimes not so excellent, jobs for their clients. The large firms (CAA, ICM, WME, UTA) have the largest number of agents (and so have the most inside information), and represent the biggest names in the business (and thus do the biggest volume of business and make the biggest deals). When all of that works in your favor, it means your agent might package your script with a huge director and an A-list actor the agency also represents, increasing the value of your script sale and the likelihood of box office success.

On the other hand, servicing those big directors and actors is the agency's priority, and they may be inclined to look out for their interests more than for yours. You might get lost in the shuffle altogether if you are not making significant money for them quickly, so don't be swayed into signing with a big place simply because of their marquee name—and that's at any point in your career. Unless you're pulling in seven-figure deals, you will always take a backseat to the high rollers. Agents at these large firms are under tremendous pressure to produce revenue for their companies. And each agent may have fifteen or twenty clients that they are constantly trying to find work for, competing with hundreds of other agents all over town for the same jobs. While there are always exceptions for anyone who writes a knockout, incredible screenplay, in all likelihood the large agencies won't be interested in someone who has just penned their first spec.

Midsize agencies (such as Paradigm, APA, and Gersh) are essentially smaller versions of the large agencies. They still have a lot of agents and represent a lot of people and make a lot of deals, but they don't have as many agents, clients, or A-listers on their rosters. They can still package scripts with their own clients or package them with the larger agencies, and can help catapult or stall out a career, just like the larger places.

For obvious reasons, the most likely spot for a new writer is at one of the boutique agencies (there are dozens) where agents don't already have a huge list of A-list clients and are more likely to be looking for The Next Big Thing. With a great logline, you may be able to get a boutique to read your script, and with a great script, to get signed. And there, you will not be one of a thousand clients looking for work. They will make more of an effort to nurture your career and not give up on you if nothing sells in the first month. They also work with the bigger agencies in terms of packaging. This can actually be an advantage, because they can go to any big agency to try to get talent attached to your script, but CAA is unlikely to go to ICM or WME if they can push one of their own clients first.

HOW DO YOU GET AN AGENT?

There's an old saying in Hollywood: Whenever you need an agent, no one wants to represent you, and whenever you don't, everyone does. Years ago, an agent at a big firm called me weekly for six months, trying to get me to sign with him. He boasted about how much more money and what better projects he could get me than my current rep. When I was finally ready to come over, he asked me what I was working on. I told him, "Nothing, that's why I'm looking to change agents." Never heard from the guy again. Similarly, I once asked a successful literary agent if he was looking for new clients and he responded in all seriousness, "No, I'm looking to steal clients from other agencies and get them writing assignments." And trying to get agents to return your phone call can be a lesson in futility. I once phoned my agent for three days straight without a reply. On the fourth day, I told his assistant my next call was to 550-4000 (a competing agency's number). He called me back five minutes later and apologized.

These are examples of why agents are sometimes viewed as arrogant, heartless, deceitful sharks (with these being their better qualities). Sadly, to many of them, a writer is merely a product, not a person, and can be tossed out and replaced on a day's notice. But before we stick any more pins into our well-coiffed, Armani-clad voodoo doll, please note. There are many honest, hard-working, compassionate agents out there who will do anything for their clients, through good times and bad, and will even return your messages within the hour.

The best way to find an agent is to write a great spec script. Two would be better, along with an arsenal of other brilliant ideas for future scripts. Agents need to know that you are talented and prolific—they're interested in a lucrative future, not just a single sale. Of course, no one will know how great a writer you are if you can't get anyone to read your script, which is the hardest thing for a new writer to accomplish. Agents don't respond to cold calls or blind submissions. There's just not enough time in the day for them to sort through hundreds of poorly written screenplays in search of that diamond in the pile of literary coal.

My first break came when a friend's mother was sitting under the hair dryer at a beauty salon in Beverly Hills. The woman sitting under the adjacent hair dryer was a literary agent. The two women started talking and the mother told the agent about her daughter's friend who had written a script. The agent offered to read it. Turns out, she was not hip to the popular music-driven youth comedies of the day and didn't know what to do with it. But her assistant had worked with some big rock bands who were repped by a large music management company that also made movies so they could put all their artists on the soundtrack. The script made its way to the head of the company. He loved it and optioned it. And my career was started.

Every successful writer has their own story of how they broke in. Some went to film school. Others worked as assistants to producers or agents. And then there are the more unique stories, such as Diablo Cody (who wrote the Oscar-nominated *Juno*) who was a full-time stripper whose blog got the attention of industry executives. Whatever it takes.

Once you do have an agent, you have to make sure you are both on the same page. That means communication has to be open on both ends. They will tell you the types of projects that are selling, send your scripts to prospective producers and executives, introduce you to everyone in town, and put you up for jobs you may be right for. You, on the other hand, must be clear about your career goals and what you want to write, let them know who your contacts are in the industry, and be willing to provide them with ample ammunition, constantly generating new ideas and new spec scripts, at least at the beginning of your career.

Also, it doesn't hurt to let your agent know you appreciate their hard work. Send them a basket of muffins or a bouquet of flowers on their birthday. A nice Christmas gift for their precious dog Sparky. And do the same for the assistant. They are the gatekeepers to keeping you on your agent's mind and getting your phone calls returned promptly. Plus, they may be running a studio one day and will remember you.

The best way to get good representation is by referral. If

somebody recommends you to an agent or manager (whose job I will discuss momentarily), suddenly you are no longer just another wannabe writer, you are a close personal friend of (fill in the blank). Your phone call will be returned and your script will be read. It doesn't mean anyone is going to like it, but at least your foot is in the door. And a referral doesn't have to come from an A-list actor, producer, or executive, though the more clout someone has in the business, the more seriously you will be taken. Anyone who truly knows the agent or manager can recommend you. It could be someone you play basketball with or who teaches you how to play the guitar, or even your third cousin's parole officer whose sister is in the biz. Just don't lie about who you know. If you say Jennifer Lawrence referred you and she didn't, then you better hope she's on a monthlong expedition to the Brazilian rainforest and cannot be reached, because the agent or manager you've called will check. And there's nothing those guys hate worse than someone who tells more brazen lies than they do.

Without that referral, however, it's a grueling grind to break in. You basically have to contact people cold, and I mean a lot of people. As mentioned, you can get a list through IMDb Pro or StudioSystem, online subscription services that list thousands of industry contacts with email addresses and phone numbers, as well as *Hollywood Screenwriting Directory*. All are updated every few months. (These sources include producers as well, and I will discuss them in the next lesson.) Most agencies and management companies state that they do not accept unsolicited material, but some do. This is where you need to entice them with that scintillating logline. Ninety-five percent of the people you contact cold will never get back to you, but you only need one responsive party. That's why you have to send out dozens of query messages. The worst thing that could happen is that more than one person is interested in your screenplay.

You may find an agent willing to represent you in a "hip pocket" arrangement. This means he read and liked your script, but doesn't have the time to take you on now as a regular client. He will, however, be willing to send the script to a half-dozen or so places and see what the response is. If someone is interested and he can make a deal for you, then he would sign you on as a full-time client. If not, you're out of luck. The advantage of this is that your script would go to top producers and be taken seriously, based on the reputation of the agent. The downside is that if no one makes any offers, your script has now been shopped around and it may be hard to find another agent to represent it once word gets out that no one was interested in it. But that's a chance you'll have to take. If you do get an offer, you'll be under no obligation to sign with this agent. In fact, since he didn't think enough of you to sign you from the get-go, your tendency might be to say, "F.U.!" But don't. This is how the entertainment business works. He got you a deal, now you're hot, and he should be gung ho to work hard to find you your next job.

You might wonder what happens if your agent leaves for another agency. Do you go with him? It would depend on his deal with his agency. Generally, you have signed with the parent agency, not the agent, so if you choose to leave and follow the agent, any new commissions for the term of your contract would still go to the first agency. However, a prominent agent may have a deal with the agency that says he can take his clients with him if he leaves. If so, then you can go and his new agency would collect the commissions on any new deals. Or you can stay with the first agency and be represented by another agent.

MANAGERS

If you can't find an agent to represent you, what can you do? That's where a manager comes in. Many writers today employ managers and you'll find they are usually more receptive to taking on new writers than agents. While their ultimate goal is the same as that of the agent—to enhance your career and help you earn a lot of money—there are a number of clear distinctions between the two jobs. Agents are focused on selling scripts and finding you work, and are more interested in the immediate success of their client. Managers want to see scripts sold and clients working, but they take a longer-term view and are more likely to work with someone to help them realize their potential, rather than wait until that potential is already completely on the page.

Like agencies, there are big management companies and small ones. Unlike agencies, managers are not licensed by the state of California and are not franchised by the WGA, so you may have to do a little more vetting than you do with agents. Yesterday she may have been working at a Ford dealership; today she's a literary manager. And as easily as they enter the business, they can exit it as well. I had a manager once who last I heard was selling lingerie at Bloomingdale's.

Also unlike agents, managers' commissions are not regulated, though they are typically 10 percent, and managers are allowed to be your producing partner—and producing your screenplay is what every manager would prefer to do. If they do produce, they won't commission your script. They will receive a producing fee and credit, and that will add much more to their bank account, as well as to their cachet. On the other hand, if it's not in your best interest to attach them as a producer on your script (e.g., there already is a producer on board), a manager should back away and simply take their commission.

Under California law, managers are not allowed to find employment for you or negotiate deals, though for new writers just starting out, especially when no one else is representing you, they just might do both. Some managers have paid a price for this as their commissions can be legally challenged later on and they can be forced to repay the commission because they got a client a job.

WHAT MANAGERS DO

Until relatively recently, very few writers had managers, but a large number do today. And at the beginning of your career, they may be the only ones willing to take a chance on you, giving detailed notes draft after draft until your script is ready to be submitted. They will give you professional advice (Should you write for TV? Should you take an assignment you're not crazy about?), forge key alliances (get you an agent and lawyer if you don't have one), manage those relationships (stay on top of the agent), and even help with personal decisions (finding you a realtor when purchasing a new home). Agents will give you their opinion, but managers give you their time.

Once your career is really launched, and you have an agent on board and the work is coming in, some writers start to have second thoughts about paying both agent and manager commissions. Ultimately, it all boils down to value received, and whether the things your manager was doing from the start continue to add value, or whether that benefit has waned, all of which is complicated by the consideration of where your career would have been without her. This is a blended question of business and loyalty that only you can answer.

Should a producer or manager want to make a deal with you, you will need to find someone to negotiate your contract. An option alone would probably not interest an agent as the commission would be too small to be worth their while. That's where our third rep comes in.

LAWYERS

The lawyer is the most respected of the three people who might represent you. Lawyers? Most respected? Only in the film business! Their job is to negotiate and review contracts. If you do have an agent to make your deal, your lawyer will also come up with things to protect your interests that your other reps might overlook. For instance, if an agency packages your script with its director or actor clients, how do you know they're not shortchanging you for the sake of their bigger earners? A lawyer will look out for just your interests. If she reps more than one involved client, she would have you sign a conflict of interest waiver, or better yet, tell you that you need another lawyer to rep you on that particular deal.

My first lawyer got me a writing assignment with a producer client of his. He told me I needed to find another attorney to negotiate my deal, and he wouldn't even recommend one because that alone would be a conflict of interest. I stayed with this second lawyer until he got into producing as well, which meant I needed to find a third lawyer in order to do business with the second one. By then I was so tired of having to find new lawyers, I was ready to hire Judge Judy (or was it Wapner back then?). Just don't hire any old lawyer who offers to represent you. It has to be someone who is well versed in entertainment law and does business on a daily basis with the business affairs departments of the major studios. If you see him on a TV commercial exclaiming, "I don't get paid unless you get paid!," move on to another attorney.

Early in my career, I optioned a script to a producer for no money. That's right, free. For two months he could take my script to any production company in town to try to set it up. After those two months, he could keep shopping it around for another year by paying me a whopping $2,500. It seemed like a crummy deal to me, but my lawyer also negotiated that I would be Executive Producer of the film and get a $50,000 fee for that if the movie got made. At the time, starving me would have gladly sold the script outright for $10,000, but the producer wasn't coughing up that kind of money.

Six months later, the producer found a small production company that was interested in the script. It was run by a former studio head who had independent financing to make movies. The thing is, he took sole Executive Producer credit on all his films. When he saw that I was Executive Producer, he flipped out. "Who the hell is this shmegegge, Andy Rose?!" The first producer came back to me and said I had to give up the credit or the company wouldn't develop the project. My lawyer informed him that the reason I gave him a free option was in exchange for the Executive Producer credit, and therefore would not relinquish it. However, we did want this production company to make the movie, and they weren't going to do so with my current deal. My lawyer then suggested a new provision. I would come down to Associate Producer credit but had to be paid $25,000 immediately and $25,000 more if the movie got made. The ex–studio head surprisingly agreed to these terms. I got my money, the production company went under, my deal with the first producer expired, I got the script back, and I optioned it to someone else a year later.

There are big law firms that have attorneys who handle entertainment law, but unlike agencies, it's the boutique entertainment law firms that have the most prestige and handle most of the A-list talent. Obtaining a lawyer is not difficult. He will charge you 10 percent commission (5 percent once you get an agent) but may want a set fee, such as $1,000, to do the initial deal. This will go against the 10 percent. After all, the initial deal may be a $2,000 option. He's not going to spend a couple hours on the phone and then read over a contract for two hundred bucks. So where will broke you with the beat-up Honda and the filthy roommates get the money to pay him? From the $2,000 you get from the option. While this may sound like a lot of money going out up front, you have just made a great contact in the entertainment industry. Your new lawyer can now help you find an agent or manager, which will be a lot easier to do now that you have a deal. Some lawyers may want you to pay them an hourly rate instead of a percentage. The problem with this is that every time you call them up to ask a question, it costs you $35. The peace of mind of being able to talk with them whenever you need to, for however long it takes, is worth paying the percentage in my book. Though if you start making a million dollars per script, reconsider.

PRODUCERS AND EXECUTIVES

A successful Italian film producer and financier didn't trust his English so he had every script he read translated into his native tongue. A writer I knew, with high hopes of selling his latest project to this producer, brought the script to his Hollywood home to be translated. When he arrived, a young woman invited him in, and the writer was immediately pounced on by an overly friendly Labrador retriever. As the writer played with the exuberant canine, the young woman commented, "I see you have took a liking to my cat." She was the translator.

PRODUCERS

Producers and studio executives hold the keys to the king-dom. They are both your greatest and most frustrating al-lies as they are the ones who hire you, but will just as quickly replace you with another writer, often seemingly for the most trivial of reasons. I was once replaced because the studio wanted a female writer to polish all the female dialogue. Perhaps they thought I was raised by Benedictine monks and had never heard a woman speak before.

If you're an established writer, you might be able to sell a script or idea directly to a studio, who will then attach a producer to the project. But in most cases, a writer gets a producer involved first (often with no money involved) before taking it to a buyer, hoping the producer's clout, enthusiasm, and connections can help make a sale. This may also include him convincing a bankable director or actor to come onboard and give the whole package even more appeal. Unfortunately, this is a double-edged sword. One studio may love the person attached, while another may have banned him from their lot. Still, a package is better than a naked script, unless the script is absolutely brilliant.

I was once introduced to an Oscar-winning producer who had an idea for a project that a well-known actress and actor had expressed interest in. This producer, however, had a horrible reputation for her extravagant dalliances with illicit chemical compounds. So bad, in fact, that she knew Betty Ford better than Jerry ever did. My agent assured me, though, that her $10,000-a-week cocaine habit was now a mere $500-a-week pot habit, which made her employable again in the eyes of the entertainment community. Not true, as I found out. After weeks of work, we couldn't set up the pitch anywhere and no one ever made a penny off it, though this producer did make a fortune a few years later writing a scathing, tell-all, bestselling book that not only named names, but ended her career in the movie business for good.

Producers are imaginative and resourceful, but sometimes a little cagey, so know who you are dealing with. As with managers (who can also be producers on your project), they are not licensed by the state so anyone can hang a shingle and call themselves a producer. If they tell you the reason they're working at Applebee's is to research a project, beware. Top producers with studio deals might have a couple dozen scripts in development at any given time, and may produce one or even two movies a year. Once they set a project up at a studio, they receive development fees to work on each one of these projects, regardless of whether they ever get made. Their payday for a "go" movie could be millions. Other producers, however, struggle to get anything set up and don't last long in the business.

I once met with a British producer who was in LA looking to set up a few new projects. He was staying at the famous Chateau Marmont Hotel on Sunset Boulevard, and I went to meet him there to see if there were any ideas we might want to take out and pitch together. I found out he had been there for two months and desperately wanted to go back to England, but he couldn't leave. Seems back then, you didn't need to pay your hotel tab until you checked out, but he had no money to pay the bill, so he had to keep staying there, and running up charges, until he sold something. At that time, he already owed $20,000. For all I know, he's still there.

Some producers will read scripts by new writers. Others will not accept any unsolicited material. Remember, established agents are sending their clients' scripts to producers every week, and many only develop a handful of new projects a year. But take note, there are development assistants who work for producers. You might have some luck contacting the lowest-ranking person (usually a story editor) at that company to read your script. After all, in order for her to climb the ladder of success, she needs to find new material, plus she's got the producer's ear.

If a producer likes your script, he may want to option it. (I will discuss what an option is in the next lesson.) Or, he may simply want to take it right into a studio and try to sell it for you without paying you a dime. In that case, you're banking on his reputation to be able to get you a deal, which should be a nice paycheck if he is successful. It could also lead to other paid writing opportunities. The disadvantage of this is that if he is unsuccessful, your script is dead meat and you've made no money. Hopefully, it will at least serve as a nice writing sample which could get you hired to write something else. And paying jobs are much more lucrative than playing the spec script game over and over again. In the beginning of your career, any writing job—even a low-paying one for a few thousand dollars—is a great opportunity to get your foot in the door and launch your career. Sometimes the experiences are rewarding, other times less so. But either way, it sure beats waiting tables, right?

I once had a producer fly me to New York for a week to

rewrite a script. My deal called for him to pay for airfare, hotel, and all my meals. He did, but the plane was one step up from the Wright brothers', the hotel was run by Norman Bates, and my first night's dinner was a can of tuna fish—chunk light, no less. All week, I sat in the hotel room and wrote my fingers to the bone. Then he was lukewarm on the script and tried to weasel out of paying me. Amazingly, the movie got made.

Conversely, another producer flew me to St. Tropez to do research on a film he had hired me to write. He paid me in advance, flew me first class, put me up in a 4-star hotel, and fed me at the finest restaurants. I spent all day on a topless beach taking, uh, notes, and all night at the Riviera's most exclusive discotheque, dancing and drinking champagne. Best part, he loved the script. Yet this movie never got made. Go figure!

Remember, no matter how enthusiastic a producer seems about your project, it's just one of many he may be juggling, along with his personal life. I once had a story meeting abruptly cut short when a producer mysteriously bolted from the room. As I later learned, he needed to get to Kmart before it closed so he could buy a weed whacker that his gardener needed the following morning. Priorities are priorities.

STUDIO EXECUTIVES

Of course, the studios are the ones that pay you and bankroll the movie, so these executives are the ones with the real power, especially the head honchos, who remind everyone of their status, including their employees. One famous studio president, who worked his underlings to death, used to tell them, "If you don't show up to work on Saturday, don't bother coming in on Sunday." Not only do these execs option and purchase scripts, buy pitches, and hire writers for assignments, but they also oversee production of the movies made for their studio. Unfortunately, nowadays, studios are not exactly open-minded in what they develop. They are corporate entities and must answer to their stockholders. And with what movies cost to make and market, they can't afford any big failures. That is why a majority of studios' slates consist of movies with built-in marketing to lower the risks. This includes comic book franchises, bestselling books, sequels, and remakes. The more daring, cutting-edge material is typically done by independent companies these days. With huge financial stakes at play, when a studio does do an original film, it's usually because of the packaging (director, actors) involved. That's why there's no need to send your new spec script to a studio executive without any elements attached, especially without representation. It'd have to be another *Citizen Kane* or *Casablanca* to be even considered. Wait a minute! Charles Foster Kane journeys to Casablanca in a tale of love, treachery, and sleds. I think I just found my next pitch.

SOMEONE IS INTERESTED

You've sent out fifty query messages and one person wants to read your script. Congratulations, you've beaten the odds! Here's what will happen next:

RELEASE FORMS

If this was a cold contact and you don't have representation, the company interested in reading your script will most likely want you to sign a release form. This is a short legal document that spells out the current relationship between you and them. It is not an agreement to do business together in any manner. That will come later if they like your script and want to proceed in working with you. In this release form, you attest that you own the material you're sending them and, most importantly, that you relieve the company of any liability should they come out with a similar movie down the line, as many comparable ideas are developed at the same time. And, if at a later date, you do think they stole your idea and made a film based on it, you agree not to sue them but go through arbitration instead. Remember though, you can't own an idea (e.g., alien comes to Earth), only the application of the idea (e.g., alien is stranded on Earth and is befriended by a small boy in a suburban neighborhood who helps him get home). You may ask yourself, "Is this a document I need a lawyer to look over?" Well, it's always a good idea to have a lawyer look over a legal document, but unless you've got a few hundred bucks to spare, you can probably read it over yourself. But read it carefully. Otherwise, some things may come back to haunt you later. Here is a copy of an acceptable release form:

Big Time Productions
6200 Hollywood Blvd., Suite 411
Los Angeles, CA 90048
Date:_____
Dear Sirs:
I am submitting to you herewith and under the terms and conditions stated herein the following screenplay (hereinafter referred to as the "Screenplay"):

TITLE: "_____"
BRIEF SUMMARY OF PLOT:

WGA REGISTRATION NO._____ NUMBER OF PAGES: _____
1. I acknowledge that you have adopted the policy, with respect to unsolicited submission of material, of refusing to accept, consider, or review such material unless the person submitting such material has signed an agreement in form

substantially the same as this. Accordingly, I acknowledge that you would refuse to accept, consider, or otherwise review the Screenplay in the absence of my acceptance of each and all provisions of this agreement ("Agreement"). I acknowledge that no fiduciary or confidential relationship now exists between you and me, and I further acknowledge that no such relationships are established between you and me by reason of this Agreement or by reason of my submission to you of the Screenplay.

2. In consideration of my execution of this Agreement, you agree to cause, within a reasonable time, the Screenplay to be reviewed and to determine whether you are interested in acquiring any or all rights in and to the Screenplay. I acknowledge that you have no obligations to me except as in this Agreement set forth, and that no other obligations exist or shall exist or shall be deemed to exist. I further acknowledge that at this time you have no intent to compensate me in any way and I have no expectation of receiving any compensation.

3. In the event that you are interested in acquiring any or all of the rights in the Screenplay, I will agree to negotiate with you in good faith with respect to your acquisition of such rights. In this connection, I understand that you may not elect to acquire any rights in the Screenplay.

4. I warrant that I am the sole owner and author of the Screenplay and that I have full right to submit it to you upon the terms and conditions stated herein. I will indemnify you from and against any and all claims, expenses, losses, or liabilities (including reasonable attorneys' fees) that may be asserted against you or incurred by you, at any time, in connection with the Screenplay or any use thereof, arising from any breach or alleged breach of these warranties.

5. I acknowledge that because of your position in the entertainment industry you receive numerous solicited and unso-

licited submissions of ideas, formats, stories, suggestions, and the like, and that many such submissions theretofore or hereafter received by you are similar to or identical to those developed by you or your employees. I agree that I will not be entitled to any compensation because of the use by you of such similar or identical material which may have been independently created by you or have come to you from any other independent source. I understand that no confidential relationship is established by my submitting the material to you hereunder.

6. Any dispute concerning this Agreement, including, without limitation, the validity or effect of this Agreement shall be litigated in the courts located in the County of Los Angeles, State of California, and both parties consent to the jurisdiction and venue of such courts, and agree not to initiate any action against the other elsewhere. At your sole election, any such dispute may be submitted to arbitration in the County of Los Angeles, State of California, in accordance with the rules and regulations of the American Arbitration Association then in effect, provided that said arbitration shall be heard before a single arbitrator, selected pursuant to said rules and regulations. Said arbitrator shall be well acquainted with the entertainment business in the County of Los Angeles. The arbitrator's decision shall be controlled by the terms and conditions of this Agreement and shall be final and binding. Judgment upon the award of the arbitrator may be enforced in any court of competent jurisdiction. The prevailing party shall be entitled to recover from the losing party, in addition to all other relief to which it may be entitled, its costs and expenses, including, without limitation, actual attorneys' fees and the costs of expert witnesses. In the event of any dispute concerning this Agreement, my sole remedy shall be to seek damages and in no event shall I be entitled to seek injunctive

or other equitable relief or undertake any legal efforts to restrict the exploitation of the Screenplay.

7. I have retained a copy of the Screenplay, and I release you from any liability for loss or other damage to the copy or copies submitted by me. I understand that your returning the Screenplay to me shall not terminate or affect any rights or obligations under this Agreement. You shall have the right, but not the obligation, to retain a photocopy of the Screenplay for your files.

8. The word "you" or "your" in this Agreement refers to Big Time Productions and any parent company, any company affiliated with it by common stock ownership or otherwise, its subsidiaries, subsidiaries of such affiliates, any person, corporation, or entity to which it is leasing production facilities, or for which it acts as a distributor or furnishes financing, and the officers, agents, servants, employees, stockholders, licensees, successors, and assigns of it and all such persons, corporations, and entities referred to in this paragraph. If said material is submitted by more than one person, the word "I" shall be deemed changed to "we" (and the corresponding verb changed to the first person plural), and this Agreement will be binding jointly and severally upon all such persons.

9. Any provision or part of any provision which is void or unenforceable shall be deemed omitted, and this Agreement with such provision or part thereof omitted shall remain in full force and effect. This Agreement shall at times be construed so as to carry out the purposes stated herein.

10. This Agreement may not be changed, modified, terminated, or discharged except in writing signed by both you and me. This Agreement, regardless of where executed or performed, shall be governed by, construed and enforced in accordance with the laws of the State of California applicable to agreements executed and to be wholly performed therein.

11. I hereby state that I have read and understand this Agreement; that no oral representations of any kind have been made to me; that there are no prior or contemporaneous oral agreements in effect between us pertaining to said material; and that this Agreement states our entire understanding. Please Note:

• Big Time Productions will not accept certified or registered mail.

• Due to the volume of submissions, Big Time Productions will not return any material.

• It will take a minimum of six weeks to read the material, please refrain from calling or contacting us before that time.

• Big Time Productions prefers scripts in standard script format not exceeding 120 pages.

• For a more efficient response on your submission, please include an email address.

_____   _____
Signature   Address

_____   _____
Print Name   Tel No.

ACCEPTED AND AGREED TO:

BIG TIME PRODUCTIONS

While most legitimate people in the film business are not outwardly dishonest (ruthless and sneaky, perhaps, but not dishonest), be aware that there are a number of unscrupulous managers and producers out there looking to prey on a young writer's desperation to get anyone interested in his or her work. They may ask you to sign a release form that gives them certain rights which you simply cannot give up. Here is an example of a release form that you must never sign.

Joe Sleazy, Literary Manager & Producer
Phone: (323)555-0490 // Email: bendover999@yahoo.com
131313 Fairfax Ave, Suite 666, Los Angeles, CA 90048

TITLE: _____
DATE: _____

WGA REGISTRATION NO. _____ NO. OF PAGES: _____

LOGLINE / BRIEF SUMMARY OF PLOT:

Dear Mr. Sleazy:
1. I am submitting to you the referenced material in consideration of your involvement as a manager & producer.
2. I agree that I am sending you this material on an exclusive basis and that while you are considering this material I will not send it to or sign with any other parties nor sign with any other representation or enter into any other third party agreements with regard to this material without your consent.
3. I agree that you shall have the exclusive right to represent it and me as a writer/creator acting as my manager for a period of two years under terms standard in the entertainment industry (10% commission). I further agree that at your option, you may attach yourself as a producer to this project (as customarily defined in the entertainment industry) and in exchange for your valuable time and involvement, your rights

as an attached producer (with a 10% ownership in the material) will continue in perpetuity on this project, while your rights as a manager are limited to a period of two years.

4. You will notify me in a reasonable and timely manner of your interest and to exercise these rights and may have me sign a standard longform management agreement with these same terms. No additional contract is needed, however, as this may serve as our entire fully binding agreement upon your notification and is not revocable by me.

5. I believe that granting you these rights will further my interests. I understand your time is valuable and you would not invest your time to consider new material without this commitment. I acknowledge and value the receipt of your valuable consideration and agree it is a fair exchange for these rights.

6. I warrant that I am the sole owner and author of said material, and/or that I have the exclusive right and authority to submit the same to you upon the terms and conditions stated herein. I will indemnify you of and from any and all claims, loss, or liability that may be asserted against you or incurred by you, at any time, in connection with said material, these rights, or any use thereof.

7. I agree that nothing in this agreement nor the fact of my submission of said material to you shall be deemed to place you in any different position than anyone else to whom I have not submitted said material.

8. I understand that as a general rule you consider literary properties through the established channels in the industry. I recognize that you have access to and/or may create or have created literary materials and ideas which may be similar to said material in theme, idea, plot, format, or other respects. I agree that I will not be entitled to any compensation because of the use by you of such similar material which may have been independently created by you or have come to you

from any other independent source. I understand that no confidential relationship is established by my submitting the material to you hereunder.

9. I have retained at least one copy of said material, and I hereby release you of and from any and all liability for loss of, or damage to, the copies of said material submitted to you hereunder.

10. I enter into this agreement with the express understanding that you agree to read and evaluate said material in express reliance upon this agreement and my covenants, representatives, and warranties contained herein, and that in the absence of such an agreement, you would not read and evaluate said material.

11. I hereby state that I have read and understand this agreement and that no oral representations of any kind have been made to me, and that this agreement states our entire understanding with reference to the subject matter hereof.

If the foregoing is in accordance with your understanding, kindly indicate your approval and acceptance by signing this agreement in the space provided below.

_____   _____

Signature   Street address

_____   _____

Print Name   City, State & Zip code

_____   _____

Telephone Number   Email address

Read sections 2 and 3 carefully. Section 2 says you agree not to send your script to anyone else while he is reading it. Well, that is absolutely ridiculous. It could take him three months to get back to you (if at all), and then there's no guarantee that he will like it. Does he really expect you to wait around all that time for his response? If so, he's more of a novice than you are. You need to get your script out to multiple people because the odds of finding someone who wants to help you is slim. If someone does show interest in your script weeks after they received it, but you're already in business with someone else—too bad. You snooze, you lose, baby!

Now look at section 3. This clause states that you're agreeing to give this person exclusive rights to represent you for two years. But what if you don't like him or his take on your script? Agreeing to do this is like agreeing to marry someone before ever meeting them on a blind date. You need to make sure you're both on the same page. Then also in section 3, he wants to attach himself to your script *forever,* earning 10 percent even if he is unable to set it up. What this will do is kill your project because after you leave this incompetent clown, no other producer will be interested in your script if this first producer, who has done nothing, gets credit and money. Bottom line is, most release forms are simple protection for a company because too many people are lawsuit-happy these days and don't understand that a lot of similar ideas are constantly circulating around.

COVERAGE

Once you sign the release and submit your script, it will most likely go first to a reader, who will write up coverage. This includes a synopsis of your script (more like a short treatment); assessments as to the quality and originality of the premise, story, characters, and writing; along with comments and a recommendation to either pass or consider, both for the material and the writer. Even though the lowest-level employee at the company often writes the coverage, it is a vital document in how your script will be perceived by those above her. Bad coverage and the person you sent the script to may not read it at all. What follows is an actual sample coverage of the script for the movie *Rushmore*, released in 1999. The names of the people involved have been blocked out for privacy reasons.

COVERAGE

READER: J*** W******
DATE: July 17, 1997
TITLE: RUSHMORE   GENRE: Coming of Age Comedy/Drama
AUTHOR: Wes Anderson   LOCATION: Private School/Large City
FORM/PP: SP/111   CIRCA: Present
SUBMITTED BY: T*** M******   ELEMENTS: Bill Murray
SUBMITTED TO: B***** B*********
LOG LINE: Consumed with a crush on a sweet teacher and various extracurricular activities, a charming 15-year-old dreamer flunks out of a private academy and reluctantly grows

up as he faces public school and vies with a quirky millionaire for the teacher's attention.

	EXCELLENT	GOOD	FAIR	POOR
PREMISE		XXX		
STORYLINE		XXX		
CHARACTERIZATION		XXX		
DIALOGUE		XXX		

RECOMMENDATION: <u>CONSIDER</u>
WRITER: <u>CONSIDER</u>

SYNOPSIS:
After fantasizing about solving the hardest geometry equation
in the world, MAX FISCHER, a pale, skinny and utterly charming 15-year-old dreamer, listens intently to MR. BLUME, a
tough-looking millionaire who's addressing the students at
RUSHMORE, a posh private day school. After Mr. Blume
advises the kids who weren't born with silver spoons to
take dead aim at the rich boys, Max compliments him on
his speech. Although Mr. Blume is impressed with Max,
DR. GUGGENHEIM, the school's headmaster, wistfully reveals
Max is their worst student. Although Max is editor of the year-
book and president of countless obscure clubs from beekeep-
ing to calligraphy, he is a terrible pupil. Dr. Guggenheim warns
Max that if he fails another class, he'll be expelled. Depressed,
Max perks up after reading a note in the margin of a Jacques
Cousteau book from the library. It's a paraphrase of a Henry
James quote that one should try to be someone on whom noth-
ing is lost. Touched, Max tracks down the last person who
checked out the book: MISS CROSS, a sweet, pretty 1st Grade

teacher. After watching Miss Cross read to her students, Max falls madly in love. When Miss Cross is sad about Latin being canceled, Max leads a petition to keep the subject even though he's been trying to get it off the curriculum for years. MAGNUS, a bully exchange student from Scotland, curses Max for making their lives more miserable.

When Mr. Blume watches his wild twin sons, RONNY and DONNY, at a wrestling match, Max charms him with his sharp wit. Max lies that his DAD is a neurosurgeon even though he's really a barber. Blume offers Max a job, but Max claims it wouldn't be fair because they would make too much money working for the same team. Later, when Max discovers Miss Cross is a widow, he claims they have a bond because they both lost someone close. Max's MOTHER died when he was 7. When Max sees the small aquarium in Miss Cross' room, he becomes obsessed with building her a huge aquarium on campus. He convinces Mr. Blume to invest in the project. Although Miss Cross delicately tells Max he's too young for her, he refuses to give up. He invites her to his play, a remake of SERPICO, but then makes a scene when she brings a young doctor, JOHN, to the celebratory dinner with Mr. Blume. When Mr. Blume apologizes for giving Max a cocktail, something sparks between him and Miss Cross.

Dr. Guggenheim expels Max after finding him with a CONSTRUCTION CREW for the aquarium project instead of in class. When Magnus cruelly accuses Max of always thinking big but never going anywhere, Max lies that he was kicked out because he got a hand job from the STACKED MOM of his chapel buddy, DIRK. Dressed in his rumpled Rushmore uniform, Max struggles to adjust to public school at Grover Cleveland High. He catches the eye of a bright Asian student, MARGARET, but ignores her. He creates a fencing club, and becomes the school's adorable mascot. When he asks Miss Cross to be his tutor, he discovers her husband, EDWARD, was the one who wrote in the Cousteau book. He gave it to her in seventh grade, and she donated it in his memory.

When Dirk sees Mr. Blume and Miss Cross holding hands, he warns Mr. Blume to stop because he'll hurt Max. When mean Magnus teases Dirk that Max is only pals with him because of his stacked mom, Dirk feels betrayed. He sends Max a note about Mr. Blume and Miss Cross. Devastated, Max yells at Miss Cross, then burns his blazer. He coldly tells MRS. BLUME about the affair, and winds up in jail after fooling with the brakes on Mr. Blume's car. Max tells Dr. Guggenheim about the affair, but then feels bad after learning Miss Cross has already resigned. When Max blames Miss Cross for getting him kicked out of Rushmore, she scares him off by wondering if a hand job would end all this so he could boast to his pals. After a brawl with Magnus, Max confronts Mr. Blume at his mom's grave. When Mr. Blume claims Miss Cross is his "Rushmore," Max wistfully reveals that she was his "Rushmore," too. As Max leaves, a rigged oak tree crashes down on Mr. Blume.

Max drops out of school, works for his dad and loses his passion for life. After visiting an ailing Dr. Guggenheim, Max learns that Mr. Blume and Miss Cross aren't together anymore. Mr. Blume thinks she still loves her dead husband. Max pretends to get hurt outside Miss Cross' house, then accuses her of dumping Blume because she's still pining for Edward. Miss Cross snaps back that Edward had more spark and imagination in one fingernail than Mr. Blume has in his entire body. When she discovers the blood is fake, Miss Cross kicks Max out.

Max is surprised when Dirk sets up a meeting between him and Margaret, the pretty girl from his class. Max apologizes for ignoring her, then smiles when she confesses her award-winning science project was a sham. A renewed Max gives Mr. Blume a makeover and leads him through the aquarium project. After penning an emotional play inspired by Mr. Blume's Vietnam experience, Max invites all his friends to see it. During the intermission, Miss Cross and Mr. Blume awkwardly talk and link arms. They watch the final act intently as Max, a wartorn recruit, kisses Margaret, who's portraying a villager. During the reception, when Mr. Blume asks Margaret to dance, Miss Cross invites Max to shake a leg. Max signals the BAND to play a slow one, then tenderly dances with Miss Cross to the oddest song of the night.

COMMENTS:

This poignant coming of age story about a 15-year-old dreamer charms from the beginning with its lively, quirky characters, sharp dialogue and moving plot. Although the theme is derivative and small, this piece deserves a look. Penned by the writers of the sleeper cult hit BOTTLE ROCKET, this comedy/drama is a surprising delight because it's so different and far more sophisticated and resonant than that raw and offbeat film. Although the hero's conflicts about bullies, girls, popularity and grades aren't original, the writers bring a fresh and witty point of view to the typical problems of adolescence. Max's crush on a teacher is sweet and painful. We get caught up in his wild schemes and plans, and root for them to succeed. The romantic triangle is believable even though it involves a 15-year-old student, a 50-year-old concrete mogul and a 20-something teacher.

Max's pranks to get back at Mr. Blume are hilarious from putting bees in Mr. Blume's hotel room to rigging a tree to fall on him. Max's wacky plays, mini-versions of popular movies, also liven the story. The only problem is that, after a while, the script feels like a series of vignettes in Max's life rather than a cohesive drama building to a climax. After Dirk sets him up with Margaret and Dr. Guggenheim remembers him at the hospital, Max's epiphany isn't powerful enough to shake him out of his depression. Although it's cute when everyone reunites for his play, Max's dance with Miss Cross somehow feels empty, like something is missing.

The vivid ensemble lifts this coming of age story above the crowd. Max is an adorable pint-sized Walter Mitty as he fantasizes about solving impossible math problems, plans a campus aquarium, writes play after play and woos Miss Cross. He is such a winning hero that it makes up for the uneven plot. The supporting cast is full of gems such as tough guy millionaire Mr. Blume and the breathtaking Miss Cross. Even the staple teen roles like the bully Magnus possess some color. While the private school setting is familiar, the writers make Max's struggle to grow up special, amusing and touching. Despite the tired coming of age premise, this comedy/drama merits consideration.

So who are these people that write the coverage? Some are professional readers who freelance for various companies and get paid per script, somewhere in the $50–$60 range. Union readers make a bit more. Other times, they are a lower-level person at a company and reading scripts is one of their job duties. Sometimes, they may even be an unpaid intern getting his feet wet in the business. Might they be knowledgeable about scripts? Perhaps. Could yours also be the first script they have ever read? Possibly. They may also love comedy but hate science fiction, which is the genre you've written. Many readers are also aspiring writers themselves and can be highly critical when assessing the competition. You see where I'm going here? You are at the mercy of the reader, because poor coverage is the kiss of death. In fact, poor coverage could mean your script never even gets read by the person you thought you were sending it to. After all, he doesn't want to waste his time reading something he has little faith in. So what is a good reader looking for?

1) **PAGE COUNT:** I've said it before and I'll say it again, the first thing anyone reading your script does is turn to the last page to see how long it is. Don't run over 120 pages. The reader will immediately think it is overwritten (too much prose), unfocused (too many characters or subplots), poorly structured (untimely plot points), has too much directing on paper (camera angles), or has not been edited (writer simply loves his work). Better to be a little short than too long.

2) **A GOOD OPENING SCENE:** A good first impression will hook a reader. Start your script with a scene that is exciting, funny, scary, or a big action event. Make the reader want to read on. Things to avoid include:

a) Voiceovers, text on screen, crawls.

b) Too many establishing shots where the protagonist tells you his life story.

c) Nonactive scenes where people are just sitting around talking.

d) Too many characters introduced right away. It's impossible to keep track of everyone.

e) Large blocks of type. Break up your paragraphs and throw in a line of dialogue if possible.

3) **AN IDENTIFIABLE PREMISE:** What is the logline of your movie? The reader has to know what the film is about by the end of Act 1, when the goal of your protagonist should be established. You can't have forty-seven pages of setup and backstory, and then first get into the movie. Also, stick to one premise per film. Subplots are fine, but don't have your hero trying to do too much. It'll only make the script seem unfocused.

4) **AN INTRIGUING PROTAGONIST:** You need an interesting hero who has a strong goal that drives the narrative, or your script will die. The audience needs to care about this character and root for him to succeed. Even if he's unlikeable, we have to be able to empathize with him and understand his quest. The protagonist should be introduced as early as possible in

the script, and it should be clear that it is his story we will be following. Don't give supporting characters too much weight in Act 1 of your script.

5) **AN EQUALLY INTRIGUING ANTAGONIST:** Remember, he doesn't have to be a person. He can also be a problem the protagonist has (drinking), or a force he needs to overcome (meteor heading to Earth). But he must be formidable enough opposition to provide ever-increasing obstacles for the protagonist. If he's a person, then he must be colorful and interesting, but not so big that he overshadows your hero. The conflict between the two must be clear and escalate as the movie goes on.

6) **SOLID STRUCTURE:** Are there three discernible acts? Are the plot points broken down into the proper timeframes of where they belong in the script? Is the goal of the protagonist established early? Does he hit his low point at the end of Act 2? Is there an exciting climax? Is everything logical and believable? Are the subplots strong but not overpowering? Will the audience leave the theater satisfied with what they've just seen?

7) **A FRESH TWIST TO ITS GENRE:** Certain elements are inherent to specific genres. That's what establishes the genre in the first place. But you can't simply rehash material

we've seen before. You must come up with a new take on familiar subject matter. What's different about your mob movie that Scorsese hasn't already done? How is your film noir murder mystery different from a Tarantino film? Come up with your own original take that's fresh and unpredictable.

8) **AN INTERESTING PLOT**: A good premise will be meaningless if you don't also have a good story. Are we able to follow the plot without getting lost or confused? Have you inserted too many flashbacks, dream sequences, out-of-order scenes, and other gimmicks in an attempt to be clever? Usually, a plot that runs like a straight line works best. Also, does the story build with each scene? Is the audience getting more and more engrossed? Above all, does the climax resolve the goal of the protagonist?

9) **A SATISFYING ENDING**: You've had months to figure out the resolution to your movie. The audience has only had ninety minutes. If they can predict it an hour into the film, then you haven't done your job as a writer. The ending must be believable and supported by what you've established in the movie, but it also must be unexpected and surprising. Also, the protagonist must achieve his goal based on his own actions and determination. No cavalry saving him. The cop must find the killer, not the cop's assistant.

The lovelorn guy must figure out how to get the girl, not have his best friend do it for him. The scientist must destroy the meteor, not his doctoral student.

10) **TIGHT, CLEVER DIALOGUE:** It must sound like the way people talk. Use wit and charm, and don't let your characters over-speak. Give everyone their own personality. Sometimes you need to use dialogue to get out exposition, but it can't sound like you're simply delivering information.

11) **TIGHT ACTION SCENES:** Action can be hard to write and even harder to read. You can't put every cut into your script or it will run two hundred pages. What you can do is put in enough short sentences to give the reader a feel of what he'd be seeing on screen, then let the director fill in the actual shots during editing. The best way to do this is to avoid long descriptive paragraphs that are hard to follow. Instead, simply list your sample shots in one or two sentences going down the page. It's much easier for the eye to follow a scene in this manner.

12) **IS THERE A MOVIE HERE?:** Is the subject matter and story suitable for filming, meaning can it be told through visual images and action, and not just dialogue? If not, would it be better off as a novel or a stage play? Can it be shot for a realistic budget, or would it

require studio financing? Is it appropriate for its target audience? You wouldn't want sex, violence, or swearing in a family movie. These are all things a writer needs to think of.

13) **AN ORIGINAL VOICE:** This is one of the intangible factors determined by your talent. Every writer has a different point of view or way of looking at subject matter. Whether it's humorous, quirky, shocking, or exhilarating, it has to be fresh, original, and unexpected.

14) **A SUCCESSFUL SCRIPT:** You've written a comedy. Is it funny? You've written a thriller. Am I sitting at the edge of my chair? You've written a horror movie. Does it scare me to death? You've written a drama. Are there tears in my eyes? You get the point here. The reader has to experience a strong emotion when reading the script and feel satisfied when they turn the last page.

I'm not saying there aren't good, fair, and qualified readers out there. There are. But you'll never know the agenda or experience of the person who first reads your script. And getting a copy of your coverage to see what they thought is not easy. Readers have been tracked down by disgruntled writers and threatened with various forms of disembowelment for panning a script.

Let's say the coverage on the script is pass, but the writer is recommended, meaning they didn't go for your story but they thought the writing was good. Don't fret. Your script may prove valuable as a writing sample. That's important because a good writing sample can help sell a pitch or get you an open assignment. But let's say the coverage was good, the person you sent the script to read it and liked it, and now wants to be in business with you. What's next?

OPTION AGREEMENT

Studios generally buy scripts, but a producer or smaller production company may offer to option it. This is a contract that allows a producer or a studio to control the rights to a screenplay for an agreed period of time (usually one to two years), for an agreed amount of money (anywhere from zero to lots depending on your leverage and the demand for the script), with the goal of making it into a film, in which case an agreed purchase price to fully own film, television, and various other rights is paid. This amount can range from five to seven figures. During this time, you cannot attempt to sell the script because you no longer own it. Legally, you're not really allowed to show it to anyone, even as a writing sample, but that is done all the time. If the movie gets made during the option period, the producer has to then purchase it from you outright. The purchase price may be in the contract ($175,000), or it may be a percentage of the budget (3 percent). There will also be some sections in the agreement on credit, profit participation, sequels, disputes, etc.

Generally, if a studio is later interested in the script, they will assume the option and make a more elaborate purchase agreement with you.

Again, if you don't have an agent and the option is too small to attract one, you *must* get an entertainment lawyer to make your deal. This contract is much more important than the release form. Once you have a lawyer, see if he can help find you an agent. It should be a lot easier now. You'll have a good referral and you just made a deal. You're hot, baby! Here is a sample option agreement:

OPTION AGREEMENT

This written agreement will confirm the basic terms between Hollywood Production Company (herein called "Producers") and Jimmy Scribe (herein called "Writer").

1. Option. For good and valuable consideration, the receipt of which is acknowledged, the Writer grants to Producers the exclusive and irrevocable right and option to purchase from the undersigned the rights to the original, unpublished screenplay entitled "Wonderful Movie" (herein called "Property") written by Writer.

Producer is granted a twelve (12) month exclusive option (herein "Option") to purchase all motion picture, television, ancillary, and exploitation rights and the customary merchandising rights to the Property. The consideration for the Option is Two Thousand Dollars ($2,000) and is due upon execution of this document.

Producers may extend the Option for an additional six (6) months upon payment of an additional One Thousand Dollars

($1,000). In addition, if the producers have obtained a development and/or production commitment, either the producers or their assignee shall have the right to further extend the option for one additional period of one (1) year for the amount of Two Thousand Dollars ($2,000).

2. Purchase price. Upon exercise of the Option or start of principal photography of the first production (theatrical, television, direct to video), whichever occurs first, Producer will pay a cash purchase price equal to three percent (3%) of the direct cost budget of the Picture. The term "direct cost budget" shall be deemed to mean the final approved (and bonded, if a completion guarantor guarantees completion) "going in" budget of the Picture, excluding all finance costs, interest charges, completion bond fees, contingency amounts and deferments.

3. Credit. Producers agree to determine the Writer's credit using the same guidelines used by the Writers Guild of America MBA.

4. Net Profits. If Writer receives sole story and screenplay credit, the producers shall pay the writers 5% of 100% of the net profits derived from any motion picture produced hereunder. In the event that Writer receives shared story and screenplay credit, said percentages of net profits will be 2.5%.

5. Sequels/Remakes. Producers shall have the right to make sequels, remakes and one or more television series based upon the screenplay optioned herein, provided that there shall have first been produced a television, theatrical or other feature length motion picture under the terms of this agreement. In the event that Writer has received sole story and screenplay credit for the motion picture, Producers shall pay Writer, with respect to any sequel, 50% of the cash sums paid with the respect to the first production and 1% of the net profits of such remake. If Writer writes the sequel, terms will be negotiated in good faith. With respect to a remake, 33-1/3% of the

cash sums paid with respect to the first production and 1% of the net profits of such remake. With respect to any television series, the per episode royalty will be in accordance with the industry standard.

6. Short Form Assignment. If Producer shall exercise the Option, Producer shall have acquired all of the Rights, and the Assignment attached hereto shall be deemed effective, and Producer may date, detach and file the same in the United States Copyright Office. Owner will duly execute, acknowledge and deliver to Producer, in form approved by Producer, any and all further assignments or instruments which Producer may reasonably deem necessary to carry out and effectuate the purposes and intent of this Agreement. If the Option is not exercised, this Agreement shall be deemed terminated and all right, title and interest in and to the Property shall remain Owner's sole property, and the Assignment shall be void.

Writer represents that he has the right to enter into and to perform this agreement and to grant all rights granted hereunder. Writer owns all rights to the Property free and clear of any liens, encumbrances, claims or litigation and Writer has full right and power to make and perform this agreement.

The parties intend to enter into a more formal agreement consistent with the terms of this purchase agreement and containing such other terms and conditions as are customary in option agreements in the motion picture and television industry.

This agreement shall be construed and governed by the laws of the State of California and the invalidity and unenforceability of any provision hereof shall not affect the validity or enforceability of any other provision.

Any disputes arising out of or relating to this agreement or any breach thereof will be settled by arbitration in accordance with the Rules of the American Arbitration Association.

IN WITNESS WHEREOF, the parties hereunto set their respective hand and seal this _____ day of October, 2017.

By: _____
Jimmy Scribe

By: _____
Hollywood Production Company

OUTRIGHT SALE

While optioning a script is great, an outright sale is better, primarily because it means a lot more money for you. And at smaller production companies, the more money they have invested in a project, the more they want to recoup that investment by getting the movie made. This may not necessarily be so at the studio level. Studios have upward of a hundred projects in development at any given time, and only produce about fifteen films a year. (They'll distribute another fifteen films that other companies have made as well.) But there's nothing like a few hundred thousand dollars in the bank to jumpstart a career and get you out of debt.

When a producer who optioned your script takes it to a studio for financing, the studio will most likely renegotiate your option contract into a writing and purchase deal. You will be paid to do a rewrite, and if they are WGA signatories, this will lead to some good money as well, perhaps

$50,000 to $100,000 for the rewrite. There is, however, one downside to going for an outright sale.

When an A-list producer gets a script from an agent or manager (or you), he often submits it to a studio without any formal agreement with the writer. That means no option money or initial deal. The reason you agree to this is because an A-list producer has the clout to get your script sold. Often, he has a deal with a studio to develop a certain number of projects a year and the studio is looking to work with him, based on his track record. So as the writer, you are sacrificing initial option money in hopes that this prestigious producer can convince the studio to buy and develop your script. Sometimes he may attach a director or actors before going in, which is called packaging. And sometimes he has discretionary funds so that if the studio passes, he can develop it anyway using his allotted money. If one studio passes, he can usually take it to others, often at the same time, unless he is exclusive to one place. The advantage of this is that you will know within a week whether your script has sold.

Okay, so what's the downside? If A-list producer takes your project to every studio in town and no one is interested, he says, "Sorry, I tried," and then drives back to his 20,000-square-foot Beverly Hills mansion in his Ferrari for a quick massage before working on the other thirty projects he's developing. Your script is now dead because everyone has seen it, and you're still driving that beat-up Honda and have three messy roommates. Basically, you have to put the script away for a year or so and then change the title and try again. Hopefully, you've been able to get this producer to refer you to an agent or manager and you get something out of this scenario.

MAKING A LIVING

Can you really give up that day job (or night job) and spend all your time just writing scripts? Once you get your foot in the door, absolutely. It doesn't mean you won't have slow years to go with the good years, but screenwriters are well paid. If you don't spend your money foolishly, like on a big house with more bedrooms than a brothel, you should be able to get past the tough times. There are three main ways that writers make a living—selling spec scripts, selling pitches, and getting hired to do open writing assignments. Let me discuss each.

SPEC SCRIPTS

Once you are established as a working writer, you may never write another spec script again. The reason for this is that so few specs actually sell, compared to the number that are submitted every week to producers and studios. Sure, if you do write a great spec and it sells, it could bring you millions, but that is by far the exception in the business. Why spend several months of your life working on a project with little chance of remuneration, if you could be working on a paid job gotten through a pitch or an open assignment?

When you're first starting out, you have no choice but to write a spec script. People in the industry need to see your ability as a screenwriter. Truth is, you'll probably have to write several specs before you have honed your craft and have one good enough to attract an agent, manager, or producer. And as previously said, even if the script does not sell, it still has value as a writing sample to hopefully get you a paying job. Obviously, if you're "between" jobs (otherwise known as unemployment), then by all means, write that spec. This may be the time to do that pet project you've wanted to write for years. But that's not the way you want to make a living as a writer.

Let's say you sold that spec script to a major studio. How much would you get? That would depend on what elements were attached, and how many companies were interested in buying it, which could set up a bidding situation. WGA minimum as of 2017 for selling an original high budget screenplay is around $136,000, but most writers get more than that. Established writers can get high six figures, and a million is not that uncommon. But let's say you, as a first-time writer, sold the script for $200,000. You would then be entitled to do the first rewrite, which could get you another $50,000. If the people you're working with like your progress, you might be hired to do another rewrite for another $50,000. All of this would go against a total bonus fee of perhaps $500,000 if the movie gets made and you get sole credit. If another writer is brought in and gets a share of screenplay credit, you would get a cash bonus of perhaps another $100,000. With no credit you get no bonus, but do get to keep everything you've been paid up till that point. I will discuss how credit is determined later in the lesson on the Writers Guild.

ASSIGNMENTS

Writing assignments are the bread and butter of the screenwriter's existence, especially at the studio level. Producers and studios are constantly looking to hire writers to work on specific projects. It might be a sequel to a movie franchise, an adaptation of a bestselling novel, a TV show being turned into a movie, an original idea from a producer that has been approved by a studio, or simply rewriting another writer on a project that is already in development. A majority of scripts developed by studios are rewritten multiple times by different writers, and each writer gets a nice paycheck for his contribution, whether or not the movie ever gets made, or if any of their work ends up on-screen if it does.

The way it works is, a studio announces an open assignment to the many agencies in town. Each agency will submit their specific writers for consideration. That writer will go in with his take on the project, and if he, the producer, and studio executive see eye to eye, he may get the job. Sometimes a producer or executive may have a writer in mind beforehand and he would have a leg up on anyone else. But remember, each studio has a hundred projects in development at any given time, so that's a lot of jobs for a lot of writers. Here is what a for-hire agreement looks like:

WRITER'S THEATRICAL CONTRACT

DATE: _____

1. NAME OF PROJECT:

2. NAME/ADDRESS OF COMPANY:

3. NAME OF WRITER:

4. WRITER'S REPRESENTATIVE:

5. COMPENSATION:

A) All guaranteed and optional compensation shall be payable one-half on commencement of the applicable writing period and one-half on delivery of the form of work.

Form of Work	Writing Period	Reading Period	Compensation
First draft screenplay	12 weeks	4 weeks	$150,000
First rewrite	6 weeks	4 weeks	$50,000

Optional:

Form of Work	Writing Period	Reading Period	Compensation
Second rewrite	6 weeks	4 weeks	$50,000

B) Additional Consideration: If Picture is produced and:

  (1) Writer Receives Sole Screenplay Credit:

    (a) Bonus Compensation: $500,000 less the aggregate of all Fixed Compensation paid pursuant to Paragraph 5 (A) above;

    (b) Participation: A sum equal to 5% of 100% of Net Proceeds.

(2) <u>If Writer Receives Shared Screenplay Credit</u>:

    (a) Bonus Compensation: One-half of the sum which would otherwise be payable pursuant to subparagraph (1)(a) above;

    (b) Profit Participation: A sum equal to 2-1/2% of 100% of Net Proceeds.

C) <u>Other Payments</u>: To the extent that payments are required by the Writers Guild of America Theatrical and Television Basic Agreement with respect to remakes or sequels for which no payment is specifically provided in the Agreement, company shall pay and Writer shall accept as full consideration therefor the minimum such payments so required by the WGA Agreement. If Writer is accorded sole "Written by" or "Screenplay by" credit, Writer shall have the right of first negotiation on all audio-visual exploitation, including, but not limited to, remakes and sequels and MOWs, mini-series and TV pilots.

6. CREDITS AND SEPARATED RIGHTS:

Pursuant to the WGA MBA.

7. PREMIERES:

If writer receives writing credit, Company shall provide Writer and one (1) guest with an invitation to the initial celebrity premiere, if held, with travel and accommodations at a level not less than the director or producer of the project.

8. DVD:

Pursuant to WGA MBA.

9. TRANSPORTATION AND EXPENSES:

If Company requires Writer to perform services hereunder at a location more than 200 miles from Writer's principal place of residence, which is Los Angeles, Writer shall be given first class (if available) transportation to and from such location and a weekly sum of $_____. ($_____ per week in a high cost urban area).

10. NOTICES:

All notices shall be sent as follows:

TO WRITER: TO COMPANY:

11. MINIMUM BASIC AGREEMENT:

The parties acknowledge that this contract is subject to all of the terms and provisions of the Basic Agreement and to the extent that the terms and provisions of said Basic Agreement are more advantageous to Writer than the terms hereof, the terms of said Basic Agreement shall supersede and replace the less advantageous terms of this agreement. Writer is an employee as defined by said Basic Agreement and Company has the right to control and direct the services to be performed.

12. GUILD MEMBERSHIP:

To the extent that it may be lawful for the Company to require the Writer to do so, Writer agrees to become and/or remain a member of Writers Guild of America in good standing as required by the provisions of said Basic Agreement. If Writer fails or refuses to become or remain a member of said Guild in good standing, as required in the preceding sentence, the Company shall have the right at any time thereafter to terminate this agreement with the Writer.

13. RESULTS AND PROCEEDS:

Work-Made-For-Hire: Writer acknowledges that all results, product and proceeds of Writer's services (including all original ideas in connection therewith) are being specially ordered by Producer for use as part of a Motion Picture and shall be considered a "work made for hire" for Producer as specially commissioned for use as a part of a motion picture in accordance with Sections 101 and 201 of Title 17 of the U.S. Copyright Act. Therefore, Producer shall be the author and copyright owner thereof for all purposes throughout the universe without limitation of any kind or nature. In consideration of the monies paid to Lender hereunder, Producer shall solely and exclusively own throughout the universe in perpetuity all rights of every kind and nature whether now or hereafter known or created in and in connection with such results, product and proceeds, in whatever stage of completion as may exist from time to time, including: (i) the copyright and all rights of copyright; (ii) all neighboring rights, trademarks and any and all other ownership and exploitation rights now or hereafter recognized in any Territory, including all rental, lending, fixation, reproduction, broadcasting (including satellite transmission), distribution and all other rights of communication by any and all means, media, devices, processes and technology; (iii) the rights to adapt, rearrange, and make changes in, deletions from and additions to such results, product and proceeds, and to use all or any part thereof in new versions, adaptations, and other Motion Pictures including Remakes and Sequels; (iv) the right to use the title of the Work in connection therewith or otherwise and to change such title; and (v) all rights generally known as the "moral rights of authors."

14. WARRANTY AND INDEMNIFICATION:

A) Subject to Article 28 of the WGA Basic Agreement, Writer hereby represents and warrants as follows:

(1) Writer is free to enter into this Agreement and no rights of any third parties are or will be violated by Writer entering into or performing this Agreement. Writer is not subject to any conflicting obligation or any disability, and Writer has not made and shall not hereafter make any agreement with any third party, which could interfere with the rights granted to Company hereunder or the full performance of Writer's obligation and services hereunder.

(2) All of the Work (and the Property, if any) shall be wholly original with Writer and none of the same has been or shall be copied from or based upon any other work unless assigned in this contract. The reproduction, exhibition, or any use thereof or any of the rights herein granted shall not defame any person or entity nor violate any copyright or right of privacy or publicity, or any other right of any person or entity. The warranty in this subparagraph shall not apply to any material as furnished to Writer by Company (unless such furnished material was written or created by Writer or originally furnished to Company by Writer) or material inserted in the Work by Company, but shall apply to all material which Writer may add thereto.

(3) Writer is sole owner of the Property together with the title thereof and all rights granted (or purported to be granted) to Company hereunder, and no rights in the Property have been granted to others or impaired by Writer, except as specified, if at all, in this Agreement. No part of the property has been registered for copyright, published, or otherwise exploited or agreed to be published or otherwise exploited with the knowledge or consent of Writer, or is in the public domain. Writer does not know of any pending or threatened claim or litigation in connection with the Property or the rights herein granted.

(4) Writer shall indemnify and hold harmless Company (and its affiliated companies, successors, assigns, and the directors, officers, employees, agents, and representatives of the foregoing) from any damage, loss, liability, cost, penalty, guild fee or award, or expense of any kind (including attorney's fees (hereinafter "Liability") arising out of, resulting from, based upon, or incurred because of a breach by Writer of any agreement, representation, or warranty made by Writer hereunder.

The party receiving notice of such claim, demand or action shall promptly notify the other party thereof. The pendency of such claim, demand, or action shall not release Company of its obligation to pay Writer sums due hereunder.

(a) Company agrees to indemnify Writer and hold Writer harmless from and against any and all damages and expenses (other than with respect to any settlement entered into without Company's written consent) arising out of any third party claim against Writer resulting from Company's development, production, distribution and/or exploitation of the Project.

15. NO INJUNCTIVE RELIEF:

The sole right of Writer as to any breach or alleged breach hereunder by Company shall be the recovery of money damages, if any, and the rights herein granted by Writer shall not terminate by reason of such breach. In no event may Writer terminate this Agreement or obtain injunctive relief or other equitable relief with respect to any breach of Company's obligations hereunder.

16. AGREEMENT OF THE PARTIES:

This document [including Attachment 1, if any] shall constitute the agreement between the parties until modified or amended by a subsequent writing.

BY: _____

PRODUCTION COMPANY

BY: _____

NAME OF WRITER

PITCH

If you have a great idea for a movie, you might try to "pitch" your story to a production company in hopes of getting hired to turn it into a screenplay. (Remember, why write on spec if someone will pay you to do the work?) I've been on hundreds of pitch meetings over the years and have sold about a dozen. Of course, the reins are a lot tighter today in terms of studios buying original ideas. When I was getting started, dozens of production companies freely bought pitches, many of which were little more than a logline. And everyone was looking to capitalize on whatever had just become a big hit.

After those *Police Academy* movies flourished in the 1980s, you could sell almost anything with a school theme. Studios developed chef school, traffic school, baker school. I was once asked if I wanted to write umpire school (I said no). Mercifully, few of these got made. And when *Die Hard* became a big hit, everyone was pitching the same story (good guy vs. group of bad guys who get picked off one by one), but in a new locale. There was Die Hard on a plane (*Air Force One*), Die Hard on a battleship (*Under Siege*), Die Hard on a mountain (*Cliffhanger*), Die Hard on an island (*The Rock*). Then someone sold Die Hard in a high-rise, which was the setting of the *original* movie. My god, they'd gone full circle!

Selling pitches is not so easy nowadays. Studios have realized that scripts just don't turn out to be what they envisioned. It ends up costing them a lot of money and they don't get what they expected in return. Instead, they are more interested in making tentpole movies based on a comic book franchise or bestselling book. Established writers can still sell a pitch, but it is based on their track record of good scripts and successful movies. However, a young writer still needs to learn the art of pitching. It is a great way to meet people in the business and to show them you have a command of storytelling, and you never know—someone may actually buy it. If they do, you would get a deal similar to the one you'd get for being hired on a writing assignment, but not as much as a spec sale. After all, with a spec sale, the buyers know exactly what they're getting. With a pitch, they only hope they know what they're getting.

So is there any correct way to pitch a story? It helps if it is "high concept" with a strong logline and a unique premise. That way, if the script turns out to be a dud, the buyer can always hire someone to rewrite you because the idea is so good. If the idea is just average and you tank on the script, there's not much to go on. Pitch meetings are also valuable because they introduce you to someone you may want to work with in the future. Even if they don't go for your idea, they have the opportunity to like you (and I don't mean in social media terms) and may hire you for an assignment down the line.

Here are some things you should do in a pitch:

1) CHITCHAT: Establish a personal relationship with some small talk before you start telling your story. Know the person's background before you meet. Do you have friends in common? Did you grow up in the same area? Did you enjoy a movie their company just made? Look for any interesting knickknacks on her

desk or items on her walls. Make her think, "This is a bright, friendly, intelligent person whom I'd like to work with."

2) **INTRO YOUR PITCH:** Make sure they know the genre and give a brief background of the story. Is it based on a personal experience? Do you know people like your main character? How did you come up with this idea? When I was a boy, my senile grandfather walked out of a nursing home unnoticed and was found hours later by a gas station attendant, three miles away. I turned this into a pitch about a missing geriatric and a mistaken identity that was well received.

3) **TELL THE PITCH LIKE YOU'RE WATCHING THE MOVIE:** Take us through each act and tell the story as the audience would see it, but not scene by scene. Just describe the characters and the main plot points. Comedy pitches should be funny, thriller pitches should have moments of surprise and suspense, dramas should be heartfelt, etc.

4) **LET THE LISTENER KNOW WHERE YOU ARE IN THE MOVIE:** Some pitches take five minutes, others twenty minutes. The listener doesn't know how far along you are unless you tell him. So use verbal cues like, "That's the end of the first act," or "At the midpoint of the movie," or "Our final scene is . . ." You don't want him to think the movie is about to end and you're still in the opening act.

5) USE VISUAL LANGUAGE: Create vivid scenes that generate concrete images and stand out in a person's mind. Avoid abstract themes and generalizations. For instance, don't say, "They have a whirlwind romance and get engaged." What would that mean on screen? Instead, say, "He flies her to Paris, takes her to the top of the Eiffel Tower, and proposes on one knee above the lights of the city." That's a scene I can see in my mind.

6) MORE CHITCHAT: End the way you began. You'll probably have a good idea of her reaction before you leave, and whether or not she's interested. But always end with some more small talk. Remember, even if she doesn't buy your pitch, you'd still like to work with this person one day, and want her to want to work with you. Now you are not just a name on a title page, you are an actual person with a face and a personality.

There are also things you should NOT do in a pitch:

7) DON'T OVERSELL: Keep the pitch conversational, like you're telling a friend a story about something that happened to you that day. Be prepared and know what you're going to say. I always rehearse my pitches many times before first going out with one. The worst thing that can happen is forgetting something important and having to go back in the story. Just don't make the pitch sound like a college lecture or an infomercial. Simply let your enthusiasm for the project shine through.

8) DON'T USE ABSURD COMPARISONS: As I said earlier, it's fine to compare your film to a style of other successful filmmakers. A Scorsese-type mob movie. A Will Ferrell–type comedy. But don't just throw out titles that don't make sense. "It's *The Treasure of the Sierra Madre* meets *American Pie*." Huh?

9) DON'T DESCRIBE EVERY SCENE IN THE MOVIE: This is instant death. It will take forever and put your listener to sleep. Stick to the main plot points and avoid subplots for now. Keep the story moving at a good pace. If the producer wants to know more, he or she will ask.

10) DON'T USE A LOT OF NAMES: Refer only to the main character by name, and use an actor's name that you see playing the part. For instance, if you think Bradley Cooper would be great for the lead, name the protagonist Brad. Then every other character is named for how they relate to him or for their role in the movie, such as Brad's girlfriend, Brad's boss, the scientist, the killer, etc. This is easy to follow. If you name your characters Joe, Melanie, Harvey, and Sue in your pitch, no one will remember who is who.

11) DON'T DISAGREE WITH THE LISTENER: Even if you hate a studio executive's ideas or suggestions, grit your teeth, force a smile, and say, "Hmm, that's interesting." You're

trying to get a job here and this may be your only offer. You'll graciously convince them of why their
dumb idea can't work after you sign the deal and cash
your first check. I had a dimwitted executive capri-
ciously suggest once during a pitch meeting that I
change the protagonist from a male to a female. In
my story, the lead was a playboy. If I went his way, the
lead became a wanton woman. "Hmm, that's interesting," I responded. No matter, he didn't buy the idea.

Just be aware that anything can happen at a pitch meeting, good and bad. When I pitched the logline of *Modern
Girls* to Universal, the executive suggested, "So it's like
Tootsie for kids," referring to the Dustin Hoffman in drag
movie. "Exactly!" I quickly responded, sensing that he re-
garded that as a positive thing. "Wait out in the hall," he
fired back. Five minutes later he called me back in to say he
had just made a deal with my agent for six figures. Unfortunately, it's never been that easy since. I once sat in traffic
for an hour to pitch to an executive in Burbank, only to have
him stop me after the first sentence to say they already had
something similar in development. Another time, I had a
great meeting where the executive loved the pitch, only to
get home and find out that he already had passed before I
had even gotten back to my car. And once, I pitched a producer my take on an idea of his, only to have him take a
call from an agent in the middle of the meeting and ask her
if she had any writers who might have a story idea for the

very premise I was currently pitching him. I guess he wasn't liking my take.

OVERALL DEAL

Though it's not as common as it once was, sometimes a studio will make an overall deal with a writer (or producer). This means they agree to hire you to develop a certain number of projects for them (perhaps two to four) and guarantee you a prenegotiated fee for each one. Some of these may be your ideas, others may be offered to you as an open writing assignment. Usually, this is a first look deal. If they pass on your project, you can take it to another studio. If they buy it, the deal is already in place.

An extension of this is what's called a housekeeping deal. Here, in addition to your preset fees, they'll provide you with offices, assistants, and pick up your expenses, but money might not change hands until you agree on a project. These deals are usually for a specific length of time (maybe one to three years) and you may be exclusive to that studio, meaning you can only work for them. In an exclusive scenario, you would be paid a salary that goes against the amounts you've agreed upon per each project. If you get movies made and are prolific, your earnings may actually exceed the minimums in your deal.

I had an exclusive, two-year overall deal with Disney at one time, and it was quite frustrating. They didn't seem to want to develop any of my ideas, and kept offering me projects

I wasn't interested in. (Space Family Robinson comes to mind.) Time kept passing and nothing was getting written. Meanwhile, they were paying me a high six-figure salary, gave me huge offices on the lot, paid for my assistant, and took care of all my expenses. In fact, the only thing they adamantly refused to give me were discounted tickets to Disneyland. (Apparently, you don't mess with Mickey & Co.) Just be aware, the money on all these types of deals is nice, but advancing your career can be just as important.

WRITING PARTNERS

Writing movies is the lonely person's profession. On a TV series (which I'll discuss in Lesson 20), you're part of a writing staff and meet every day, collaborating on outlines, scripts, new characters, future episodes, etc. Every show has to be written, shot, and delivered to the network by a certain date and the pace can be quite hectic. But feature films seldom have these kinds of deadlines. Once you're hired on a project, you head off to write your script and you turn it in when it's done, usually about twelve weeks later. You rarely work closely with a producer or director in the early stages, so nobody is checking up on you or prodding you along. And if you're working on a spec script, nobody, except perhaps your landlord who's waiting on your rent check, cares if you finish at all. This kind of writing requires a lot of self-motivation and discipline. You may experience writer's block and be tempted by a plethora of enticing distractions such as the internet, the TV, the stereo, your smartphone, the shopping mall, the refrigerator, and my favorite, the beguiling afternoon nap.

This is where a writing partner can be beneficial. There are many advantages to working with someone on a daily basis. Each of you motivates the other and helps push the project along, talking through plot points, character development, dialogue, subplots, etc. This is especially crucial if you have different, but complementary, talents. You may be great with structure and action, but she's great with dialogue. Together, you've got all the bases covered. A writing partner also gives you someone to celebrate your successes with, as well as someone to commiserate with during the down times.

On the minus side, you'll reduce your paycheck by half, argue over creative differences, and risk doing the bulk of the work while sharing the credit equally. That's why it's important when working with a partner to make sure your relationship is defined from the get-go. And to prevent any misunderstandings, define this relationship in writing through a collaboration agreement in case problems arise down the line, particularly in terms of credit and money.

I had an oral arrangement with a writer on a script we rewrote and produced together in which I would get first position on the writing credit, and he'd get first position on the producing credit. Problem was, we lost a WGA arbitration hearing (which I will discuss in the next lesson) and didn't get *any* writing credit. Since I had done almost

all of the work on the script, along with the bulk of the producing, I felt I deserved first-position producing credit, as
it would be our only credit on the film. He tried to hold
me to our original agreement. Ultimately, the studio decided the credit positions and put me first, all of which soured
the partnership.

In another instance, I wrote a script based on an idea of
another writer. I would take sole screenplay credit, and I assumed we would share a story credit as I came up with
most of the major plot points on my own. You know what
they say about the word "assume"? (It makes an "ass" out of
"u" and "me.") Turns out he insisted on sole story credit and
30 percent of the sale price. While I found this to be outrageous, we had not made an agreement beforehand so I was
stuck. Either agree to these terms or toss the script and
get nothing after my months of work. The moral—get it in
writing!

What follows is a sample of a formal screenwriter's collaboration agreement. But you and your partner could draw
up a much simpler one as well. Just make sure you include
the credit each one of you will receive, the order of names
in the credit, who will get what percentage of the total fees
earned, and what agent, if any, is going to represent the
project.

SCREENWRITER'S COLLABORATION AGREEMENT

This agreement is by and between:

_____and_____

_____, hereafter referred to as the "Parties" and "Co-Writers" and whose contact addresses for purposes of this Agreement are as follows:

Co-Writer Name, Address, Phone, Email:

_____

_____

Co-Writer Name, Address, Phone, Email:

_____

_____

The Parties are about to write in collaboration on a screenplay, hereinafter referred to as the "Work" and with a working title of "Apple Pies," which is based on:

_____

In consideration of the execution of the Agreement, and the undertakings of the Parties as hereinafter set forth, it is agreed as follows:

1. The Parties shall collaborate in the writing of the Work and upon completion thereof shall be the owners of the Work in the following percentages:

Co-Writer Name and Percent _____: _____%

Co-Writer Name and Percent _____: _____%

2. Upon completion of the Work it shall be registered with the Writers Guild of America, West (WGAW) or Writers Guild of America, East (WGAE) as the joint work of the Parties. If the Parties agree that additional registration of the Work with the United States Copyright Office is necessary, both Co-Writers are to be listed as authors of the Work and as copyright claimants of the Work, and their names are to be positioned as indicated in Paragraph 5.

3. If, prior to the completion of the Work, either Party shall voluntarily withdraw from the collaboration, which withdrawal must be confirmed in writing, then the other Party shall have the right to complete the work alone, or in conjunction with another collaborator, and in such event the percentage of ownership, as set forth hereinabove in Paragraph 1, shall, if requested by either Party, be revised by a written amendment agreed to by both Parties. The continuation of the Work by the other Party shall occur only with the consent of the Party legally owning or controlling any preexisting material upon which the Work is to be based, including, but not limited to, a completed outline, treatment, script, book, short story, article, photograph, video, film, sound recording, artwork, or life story.

4. Either Party may terminate this Agreement prior to completion of the Work, effective with the giving of written notice of termination, in the event that the other Party commits a material breach of its obligations, and the breach is not remedied within 30 days of receipt of written notice of the breach requesting its remedy. Such aforesaid notice of termination shall be filed with the Writers Guild of America, West (or East), if one or both Parties are members. The failure of a Party to enforce any provision of the Contract shall not constitute a waiver nor affect its right to enforce such and every other provision.

5. Any contract for the sale or other disposition of the Work, where the Work has been completed by the Parties in accordance herewith, shall require that the writing credit be given to the authors in the following manner:

by _____ & _____.

6. Neither Party shall sell, or otherwise voluntarily dispose of, the Work, or their share therein, without the prior written consent of the other, which consent, however, cannot be unreasonably withheld.

7. Each Party shall keep the other Party informed in a reasonable and timely manner in matters and required mutual decisions regarding the Work. Each Party shall respond to communications from the other Party regarding the Work and from others having an interest in the Work in a reasonable and timely manner so as not to harm or unreasonably delay the creation, sale, or other disposition of the Work.

8. It is further acknowledged and agreed that _____ shall be the exclusive agent or representation of the Parties for the purpose of sale or other disposition of the Work or any rights therein, until such agent or representation is terminated by the Parties, or ceases to represent the Work for any reason. In the absence of an agent or other representation, all said payments are to be made directly to the Co-Writers in the percentages stated in this Agreement. If no agent or representation is available at the time of signing of this Agreement, the phrase "Representation information not available at the time of signing" shall be written in the space above provided.

9. Expenses of any amount for which the Parties are mutually responsible shall be incurred only with prior written mutual consent. Either Party may elect to absorb an expense in order to advance the production or promotion of the Work and in such instance the Party making the expenditure cannot later require full or partial compensation for such expense from the other Party.

10. All money or other consideration whatsoever derived from the sale or other disposition of the Work shall be applied as follows:

(a) In payment of commissions, if any,

(b) In payment of any expenses or reimbursement of either Party for expenses paid in connection with the Work,

(c) To the Parties in proportion of their ownership.

11. It is further understood and agreed that, for the purposes of said Agreement, the Parties shall share hereunder, unless

otherwise stated herein, the proceeds from the sale or any and all other disposition of the Work and the rights and licenses therein and with respect thereto, including but not limited to the following:

(a) Motion picture rights

(b) Sequel rights

(c) Prequel rights

(d) Remake rights

(e) Television rights

(f) Radio rights

(g) Book and other media publication rights

(h) Interactive rights

(i) Any other computer-related or new media-related rights.

(j) Merchandising rights

(k) All other rights now known or known in future

12. Should the Work be sold or otherwise disposed of and, as an incident thereto, the Parties—or either of them—be employed to revise the Work or write another media presentation thereof, the total compensation provided for in such employment agreement shall be shared by the Parties hereto in the same proportion as their ownership as set forth hereinabove in Paragraph 1. If either Party is requested to be involved in such revision but shall be unavailable for collaborating therein (which unavailability shall be evidenced by a written confirmation thereof, signed by such unavailable Party), then the Party who is available shall be permitted to do such revision and shall be entitled to the full amount of compensation in connection therewith.

13. If either Party hereto shall be employed in any capacity other than in connection with the rewriting or revision of the Work (e.g., as an Associate Producer), then the other Party shall not be entitled to either any compensation or credit in connection therewith.

14. If either Party hereto shall desire to use the Work, or any

right therein or with respect thereto, in any venture in which
such Party shall have a financial interest, whether direct or in-
direct, the Party desiring to do so shall notify the other Party
of the fact and shall afford such other Party the opportunity
to participate in the venture or in the proportion of such other
Party's interest in the Work. If such other Party shall be un-
willing or unable to participate in such venture, such other
Party shall have no further right of participation, or to any compensation arising therefrom, other than their proportionate
share in the sale or other disposition of the Work to such a
venture at it's fair market value which, in the absence of mutual agreement of the Parties, shall be determined by arbitration in accordance with the regulations of the Writers Guild of
America, West (or East).

15. Each Party hereto warrants and represents to the other
that any material written or provided by him or her in connection with the Work is not in any way a violation of a copyright or common law or right of privacy and that it contains
nothing of a libelous or illegal character, and each party
agrees to indemnify and hold the other harmless against
any loss or damage arising out of a breach of any of the foregoing warranties and representations described in this
clause.

16. Said Agreements shall be executed in sufficient number of copies so that one fully executed copy may, and
shall, be delivered to each Party, the agent representing
the Work (if available), and the Writers Guild of America,
West (or East). If any disputes shall arise concerning the
interpretation or application of said Agreement, or the
rights or liabilities of the Parties arising hereunder, such
disputes shall be submitted to the Writers Guild of America, West (or East), if one or both Parties are members, for

arbitration in accordance with the arbitration procedures of the Guild. The determination of the Guild arbitration committee as to all such matters shall be conclusive and binding upon the Parties.

17. The terms of this Agreement shall be in effect continuously with the life of the Work.

18. Notices by mail shall be addressed to each Party's address as given above, or to such other address as such Party may hereafter specify by notice duly given.

19. Each Party shall endeavor to keep the other informed of any change of contact information regarding this Agreement, but failure to do so, or in a timely manner, shall not affect the terms of this Agreement.

20. The terms and conditions of this Agreement shall be binding and inure to the benefit of the executors, administrators, and successors of each Party, whose respective signatures herein below shall constitute this to be a complete and binding Agreement between them. This Agreement may not be assigned or modified by either party without the prior written consent of the other. Any of the terms and conditions of this Agreement may be modified by a written amendment signed by both Parties.

21. The Parties shall have the right to make known or reference the occurrence of this collaboration, even if sale, option, or other disposition of the Work does not occur. There is no time limit imposed in efforts to achieve the sale, option, or other disposition of the completed Work. This document, including any attachments and signed amendments, is the entire agreement between the Parties.

ACCEPTED AND AGREED this _____ day of _____ _____, 20_____.

_____

_____

Signature   Signature

_____

_____

Co-Writer Printed Name   Co-Writer Printed Name

Once you do decide to work with someone, you must consider how the two of you will work together and who will be doing what. Will you sit in a room across from each other and go over everything line by line? Will one partner write a scene on his own, then have the other partner go over it? Does one person take the lead with dialogue and the other with action? It's imperative that each person feels the other one is making a fair contribution or resentment will build quickly. When that happens, the pressure of working together will be much worse than that of working alone.

There have been many successful writing teams over the years. Some partnerships have lasted decades and produced numerous successful films. Billy Wilder and I.A.L. Diamond had a string of hits in the 1950s and 1960s (*Some Like it Hot, The Apartment, The Fortune Cookie*). Lowell Ganz and Babaloo Mandel wrote many of director Ron Howard's early films (*Nightshift, Splash, Parenthood*). Ted Elliott and Terry Rossio have hit more recent pay dirt (*Little Monsters, Shrek, Pirates of the Caribbean*). And the brothers Farrelly (*Dumb and Dumber, There's Something About Mary*) and Coen (*Fargo, The Big Lebowski*) have had much success with their particular styles of irreverent comedies.

I had a full-time writing partner early in my career. He was my complete opposite—a loud, portly, funny, brilliant, well-read, street-smart high school dropout from Greenwich Village who had wanted to work in the movie business since he was a kid. We met in one of those writing classes that I spoke of earlier. As he told me later, he was trying to figure out a furtive way to steal some of my ideas when it occurred to him it would be much easier to just work with me instead. I knew nothing about the movie business at the time so I said, "Sure."

This new partner was not a great writer, but he was a great salesman and even at just twenty-two years of age, he understood what the then current market was in Hollywood and how to make contacts, open doors, and sell scripts. All he needed was material, and I was a good enough scribe to provide it. The way we worked was, I wrote pages, he edited them, I rewrote them. We barely spent time together because I was a day person and he was a night person. This went on for several weeks until we finally had our first full-length script. It was a teen comedy called *Play Money* about a group of boys at a boarding school who find $10 million that's fallen out of a plane and go nuts spending the cash. I took screenplay credit, he took story credit, though after this project we split all credit and money equally.

Through some of his late-night connections, the script found its way to a small production company that wanted to option it. We found a lawyer to make our deal, and through the lawyer, a boutique literary agency that was becoming a household name in the industry. Within weeks, we were selling projects to major studios. Everything went well with the partnership for a couple of years until the distribution of duties started to become skewed. I found that I was doing all the work and my partner was doing all the drugs. And drugs lead to outrageous behavior, which in turn, alienates people and frightens off prospective employers. What kind of outrageous behavior, you ask?

He stuffed a large sock into his pants when we were pitching to a high level studio executive whom we knew happened to be gay, in hopes of impressing him with more than just our idea. (We did not get the deal, though I believe my partner got a dinner invite.)

He wore fuzzy bear-claw slippers to a formal dinner at a 5-star restaurant with Madonna, whom we were trying to sell an idea to, thinking she would get a kick out of it. She didn't and bolted from the project before the main entrée even arrived.

He disappeared with a script he had been working on the day it was due because he hadn't written anything, figuring the production company would be willing to wait. They weren't and I had to write the whole thing in a week while on vacation or return $50,000 that we had been paid.

He stole an official seal from a judge's chamber during a shoot at a courthouse as a souvenir because he didn't think anyone would miss it, then denied he took it. The judge was furious and forbade that any city, county, or state permits for shooting be issued to the studio until he got it back.

When the president of the studio threatened to cancel our $750,000 overall deal, my partner quickly returned it.

He flipped his brand-new BMW onto its roof while inhaling nitrous oxide as he raced down Melrose Boulevard and had to be pulled from the car by paramedics. Surprisingly, they didn't care about the cause of the accident and even asked if he'd like them to remove the tank before the cops arrived. Apparently, this was a common occurrence in LA.

As you can see, not all partnerships work out in the long run. Yet when starting out, we worked well together and would not have had the same opportunities or success had we been on our own. In other words, if you can find someone you're compatible with, it might be worth a try. At least until you're ready to kill them.

THE ALMIGHTY WGA

While new writers will write for anyone with a checkbook (or cold, hard, under-the-table cash), ultimately, every screenwriter wants to become a member of the Writers Guild of America, a labor union formed to represent and protect the interests of its members who write movies, television shows, and internet content. The WGA negotiates a collective bargaining agreement—known as the Minimum Basic Agreement, or MBA—with studios, networks, and major independents. It is renegotiated every three years before its expiration. This contract establishes agreed-upon creative rights, minimum compensation, health insurance and pension contributions, credit determination, and payments of residuals, among other things.

Every company, large and small, who wants to hire a WGA writer agrees to abide by the MBA, and WGA writers can only work for signatories or face stiff fines. In addition, the WGA resolves disputes between its members and producers (e.g., over compensation) and between fellow members (e.g., over credit on a screenplay that was rewritten), provides educational seminars, a bimonthly magazine, and even holds screenings of current movies at discounted prices at their private theater in Los Angeles. Oh, and let's not forget about their annual Christmas party. My advice regarding that soirée—avoid the shrimp.

REGISTRATION

One service that's available to both members and non-members provides documented registration of your work. For a fee (currently $10 members, $20 nonmembers), you can send your material in to the Guild, electronically or hard copy, and have it securely stored for a period of five years. You will receive an official registration certificate that lists the title of your work, type of content, and names of authors for the material you are submitting. This certificate verifies what was sent in and the date it was submitted, should any problems arise down the line about ownership of the property. You can register screenplays, teleplays, treatments, as well as books, stage plays, poems, lyrics, drawings, and music. Truth is, you can register anything since nobody at the Guild reads what you send in; they just store it. Registration with the WGA, however, is not the same as registering with the United States Copyright Office. While you already have certain copyright protections once you write a screenplay, registering it with the Copyright Office gives you some additional statutory remedies. A copyright lasts for your entire lifetime plus seventy years, just in case there's a deal to be made in the hereafter once you kick the bucket. (Word is, Saint Peter loves a good thriller.)

MINIMUMS

Under the MBA, the Guild and producers have agreed to certain set minimum payments a writer must receive when working for a signatory company. (The MBA itself and those minimums are posted on their website: wga.org.) These minimums include payments for screenplays, treatments, rewrites, and polishes on feature films, based on the budget of the film, as well as minimums in television. In 2017, minimum payment for an original screenplay was about $136,000 for a budget over $5 million. Under that budget amount, the minimum was around $73,000, though these figures rise yearly. A non-Guild writer working for a non-signatory company would get significantly less, while a new writer working for a signatory company would probably get close to scale. However, a highly sought after script could fetch way more. Again, these are just the minimums producers can't pay less than to a WGA writer. Once you are established in the community, you would receive significantly more than minimum. Many top writers receive seven-figure paydays for a script, and if more than one studio is interested in a project, a bidding war can develop and that number can become several million dollars.

CREDIT

Receiving on-screen credit is crucial to a writer. Not only does it guarantee you residuals down the line, but it determines how much, if any, of your production bonus you are entitled to receive (which could be worth hundreds of thousands of dollars as well). In addition, it adds accolades to your résumé, which helps in securing future jobs and raising your writing fees. If you are the only writer to work on an original script, you will get sole "written by" credit. But sadly, this is the rarity in Hollywood. Most movies are written and then rewritten by two, three, or even as many as twelve subsequent writers. While this is great in terms of providing a plethora of paid writing assignments to Guild members, what you often end up with is a compilation of first drafts that don't enhance the original script, but rather turn it into an unrecognizable mess and a bad film. Some writers are replaced because they simply run out of ideas. Other times the director or lead actor has a favorite writer he likes to work with and wants his input. Sometimes the studio owes a writer a favor and hires him. So with all these writers working on one project, how is credit determined?

The production company makes the initial determination on whom they feel deserves credit, based on the contributions of all the writers who worked on the script. Back in the pre-Guild days of the 1930s and 1940s, that's the credit that stood. Fortunately, things are now different. Any writer who worked on the script can request an arbitration hearing, conducted by the Writers Guild, if they are unhappy with the studio's determination. If any writer is also a producer or director on the film, this hearing is automatic. Three WGA arbiters read every draft written for the movie and compare it to the shooting script. Then they individually decide which writers they feel deserve what credit, based on the policies of the Writers Guild Credits Manual. (There is a manual for feature film credits and another one for television credits, though both are similar.) A maximum of three writers can get screenplay credit, so as not to overly dilute the value of credit, though a writing team is considered one writer. If all the arbiters agree, then that is the final credit. If none can individually agree, then they talk it over to discuss their reasoning. In the end, majority rules.

Basically, credit is decided on a holistic basis, taking into consideration dramatic structure, characterization, dialogue, and original scenes. Changing apples to oranges means nothing. The first writer's script carries the most weight. On an original screenplay, any subsequent writer would need to change 50 percent of the script to receive any credit. It's a third of the script on an adaptation. Of course, writers know this, so in order to try and get credit, some scribes will needlessly change things from previous drafts that work well simply to add more of their own contribution. This is one reason more writers on a project does not mean a better script. On an original screenplay, a shared "story by" credit is the lowest credit the first writer can get, though it can also mean a writer simply wrote the story to the film but did not work on the actual script. "Written by" credit is given when the same writer is entitled to both screenplay and story credit. "Screenplay by" credit is given when there is source material of a story nature. When doling out residuals, the screenplay writers divide up 75 percent of the money and the story writers get 25 percent. It's easy to tell if more than one writer worked on a movie. Let's say the credits read:

Screenplay by Bill Shakespeare & Chuck Dickens and
Eddie Allan Poe
Story by Eddie Allan Poe

The ampersand signifies a writing team, and they would be considered one writer. The "and" denotes a separate writer working independently of the others. In the case above, Eddie Allan Poe probably wrote the original script. Then the writing team of Shakespeare & Dickens rewrote him and changed at least 50 percent of the script, though probably more to warrant first position screen credit. However, Poe wrote the original story, so he got sole story credit. There may have been other writers on this project as well (Ernie Hemingway? Billy Faulkner?), but they didn't contribute enough to earn any credit. When the residuals are divvied up, the Shakespeare/Dickens team will split 37.5 percent of the money, and Poe will get 37.5 percent plus 25 percent for his story credit. Please note that even the best A-list writers are rewritten on a regular basis, so there is no shame in being taken off a project. Sometimes it is actually a relief, depending on who you've been working with. And there are times when a subsequent writer actually does enhance the script. There have even been cases when writers sharing credit meet for the first time when they're collecting their Oscars at the Academy Awards.

RESIDUALS

One of the most important services the WGA provides is collecting residuals from the many production companies selling shows and movies in what are called "supplemental markets"—the venues that follow the theatrical release of a movie or the broadcast of a television movie. Residuals are the additional compensation writers receive from revenue generated after the initial use of their material. In the feature film business, this includes DVD sales and pay, cable, and free television. For a television show, syndication and international broadcast sales would also be included. The exact formulas used by the Guild to calculate residuals can get very complicated, but they do keep track of and audit all the money collected by these various companies. Paid quarterly, residuals are the lifeblood of the writer who is "between jobs." A successful movie or TV show can generate hundreds of thousands of dollars in extra income to a writer over the course of many years. But note, just because you worked on a script doesn't mean you will get any residuals. To do so, you have to receive on-screen writing credit, as determined by the process previously discussed.

MEMBERSHIP

It's not easy to become a member of the Writers Guild. Many years ago, simply selling a one-sentence story idea for any type of content under their jurisdiction was enough to get you in. But the Guild soon realized that too many non-writers were joining the ranks of real writers and came up with a point system to determine who qualifies. Basically, you need twenty-four points in a three-year period to become a member. Different types of projects merit different numbers of points. For instance, selling or being hired to write a feature-length screenplay is worth the full twenty-four. A rewrite on a feature script would be worth half that. Coming up with a feature story is also worth twelve points. Scripting a thirty-minute TV show nets you six points; a sixty-minute show, eight points. But remember, the company paying you has to be a signatory of the Guild or none of this will count in terms of accruing the necessary points to join. On average, the WGA admits about three hundred new members each year. If you are admitted, you pay an initiation fee of $2,500, $100 a year in dues, and 1.5 percent of your earnings from covered writings. Once a member, you are entitled to pension and health benefits (eligibility determined by recent income), as well as legal protection.

I once was hired to write a script and received my start-up money, but before I finished the first draft, the company decided to drop the project. They also decided not to pay me what I was contractually owed had I turned in the finished script. I didn't need to sue them. I just contacted the Guild, who threatened to put them on their unfair/strike list, which would prevent any other WGA writer from working for them. And if that didn't work, the Guild would sue them and handle the legal fees. A week later I got my final check.

WHAT THEY DON'T DO

While it's important to know what the Guild will do for you, it's equally important to know what they *don't* do. They don't help get you work and they don't help you find an agent, which are, unfortunately, the two things a new writer needs most. On the other hand, unlike the United Auto Workers or Teamsters, seniority means nothing in this union, so fresh talent can make as much money as seasoned scribes. (With age discrimination rampant in Hollywood, often more.) The Guild does have numerous committees for its members to participate in, such as the LGBT Writers Committee; a number of programs like the Showrunner Training Program; and online advice columns such as one on new technology, all to aid members in advancing their careers. To learn more about the workings of the Guild, check out their website. There are sections for members, employers, contract information, a guide to the Guild, news, events, and more. Then get back to your script so you can sell something and join one day.

SOFTWARE

A long time ago in a galaxy far, far away, people wrote their screenplays on a prehistoric mechanical contraption known as the typewriter. I had one when I first started out—a Smith-Corona Coronet Super 12, one of the true workhorses of electric typing machines. But then, thanks to guys like Bill Gates and Steve Jobs, the personal computer found its way into our homes and offices, revolutionizing the way we write today.

Now, nearly everyone with a heartbeat uses some sort of word processing program to compose all their written documents. And while Microsoft Word has become the standard for basic text, a few other programs have emerged as industry standards for writing screenplays, both on PCs and Macs. All of them do the basic formatting for you, capitalizing script elements such as scene headings and transitions, wrapping the dialogue margins sooner than the action margins, numbering the pages automatically, etc. The only real differences are the bells and whistles that each software company adds to entice you to buy their product. Some offer templates for screenplays, teleplays, and stage plays; the ability to save as a PDF (most important); scene breakdown cards; note panels; production and revision modes; collaboration capability; spellcheck and thesaurus; import/export features for other software; and technical support, to name a few.

The two most popular programs are Final Draft and Movie Magic Screenwriter. They list for about $250 but are usually discounted. If you're enrolled in school, an educational version (which is the basically the same as the standard version) can often be purchased for about half that. Still, $125 is a lot of money for many cash-challenged students who are just getting their feet wet on screenwriting and may not pursue it professionally. That's where a program like Celtx comes in. Currently, this basic screenwriting formatting software is offered for FREE, which will save you lots of money better spent on cronuts, lattes, and a superior data plan. Granted, it doesn't come with many of the enhancements the other programs have, but it's enough to get you started and enable you to turn out a professional looking script. Before you make any decisions, however, check out the websites for all these programs and see what works best for you, and the current prices.

Besides formatting software, a number of programs are also available to help you write your script. Among these are Dramatica, Contour, StoryO, Persona, Scrivener, Master Storyteller, and countless others. But are they effective? Will they really help you write a masterful script that can sell? That depends on your expectations. No program is a substitute for imagination, so don't think investing a couple hundred dollars into modern technology is going to turn hamburger into prime rib, or a weak story into an award-winning masterpiece. However, for a novice writer, inexperienced with structure and character growth, this kind of software may help you organize your thoughts better, and keep you on track and focused in the development of your script.

The way most of these "creative" programs work is to ask you a series of questions about your story and characters and then guide you, step by step, in creating a linear narrative and a number of possible character relationships. They may help frame your story, which can be valuable to a new writer, but no program is going to come up with intriguing plot twists and scintillating dialogue. That's where your abilities and talents as a writer come in. Shakespeare didn't use software, and neither did Hemingway, Fitzgerald, Salinger, or Tolkien. And just as helpful as these programs can be, they can also become a crutch if you rely on them too heavily at the expense of just thinking things out. In addition, much of this software has steep learning curves, eating up time that could be better spent simply writing the darn script. My advice, try a demo and see if it makes sense to you before opening up your wallet.

However, the formatting software I first mentioned is a must and will make you a better writer. In the old typewriter days, no one wanted to change a description or add a line of dialogue because it meant a lot of whiting out, cutting and pasting, using A and B pages, or having to retype an entire page. Writers would resist making changes to avoid this and the scripts suffered. And trying to write a screenplay using Microsoft Word can be difficult as well, especially with different margins for all the different script elements. Remember, the easier it is to rewrite, the better the writer you'll be. And the easier the software is to use, the better the writer you'll be as well.

TV WRITING

While this is a book on feature film writing, it would be remiss of me not to devote one lesson to writing for the small screen. Every writer nowadays should be able to do both. That wasn't the case when I first got started years ago. Back then, you were either a movie writer or a TV writer and there was very little crossover. A feature film career was seen as more creative and prestigious, while a position on a television show was more the job of the hired journeyman. Boy, have things changed.

TV VERSUS FEATURES

The proliferation of quality cable channel programming and imaginative internet shows has reversed the perception of the two mediums. Today, feature films, at least at the studio level, are mostly a hodgepodge of ridiculously high-budget sequels, remakes, superheroes, old TV shows, bestselling books, and pet projects of A-list stars. While no major studio aims to make a bad movie, keeping the stockholders happy is paramount (pardon the pun) to these companies, and quality has become secondary to box office gross. Fortunately, the independent filmmaking world has filled in these abandoned holes and is turning out inventive product at a reasonable cost. If you're unsure which films are theirs, just look to see what is nominated for Best Picture Academy Awards every year. It ain't *Spider-Man 7*.

Television, however, has come a long way since the days of broadcast network dominance, before cable TV, DVDs, and internet competition whittled away their audience. In the late 1970s, 90 percent of all American households were watching one of the three main networks—CBS, NBC, or ABC (FOX didn't commence until 1986)—during prime time, which is 8:00 P.M. to 11:00 P.M. Today, it's closer to 40 percent. Your basic cop, doctor, lawyer, family, sitcom, and reality-based shows still air on these networks. But in the past twenty years, groundbreaking series that would never have had a chance on broadcast television have swarmed pay channels such as HBO and Showtime; basic cable channels like A&E, Bravo, FX, AMC, TNT, SyFy, and MTV; and digital channels like Netflix, Amazon, and Hulu. Series like *The Sopranos, Sex in the City, The Walking Dead, Breaking Bad, Dexter, House of Cards, Curb Your Enthusiasm,* and *Orange Is the New Black* have taken television writing to levels never seen before. So even if writing the feature movie is all you really want to do, you can't ignore the many opportunities to work in TV. And remember,

90 percent of the feature scripts developed at the studio level never get made, and those that do may be in development for years. With television, once a series is picked up, 90 percent of the scripts written for that show will get made, and quickly. Each show has an air date and episodes need to be written, shot, edited, and locked before then. In general, the only time a written TV script for a series isn't shot is if the show gets canceled before production begins. (Note: this does not apply to pilot scripts. Most ordered up by a broadcast network are not picked up as a series.)

WHO'S IN CHARGE

There are other reasons to delve into television as well. In features, the director is king and is often seen as the holier-than-thou auteur of the film. Working with the production company, he approves the script, casts the actors, picks the locations, hires the cinematographer and editor, shoots the movie, selects the music, and has final say in what the end product looks like (within reason, of course). Oh, he also can replace you as the writer if he so chooses. And even if he doesn't, your job is usually done before the first day of principal photography. Your next involvement on the movie may be walking unnoticed up the red carpet at the gala premiere, and then only if someone in the film producer's office remembered to invite you.

In television, however, the writer is the almighty king, emperor, head honcho, all powerful grand poobah and lord of the flat-screen. You see, most writers on any given show are also the producers whose names appear in the opening credits. The Executive Producer is usually the creator of the show and often the showrunner. He is in charge of everyone and needs to make sure everything gets done on time and the show is delivered to the network on schedule. (There may be nonwriting Executive Producers as well, who may be executives of the production company or managers of some of the talent.) Below the showrunner is the writing staff with titles and a pecking order of Co-Executive Producer, Supervising Producer, Producer, Co-Producer, Story Editor, and Staff Writer. The director in series television works under the showrunner, brought in to direct the script that's already locked, cast, and ready to go. Under watchful eyes, he shoots for a week or so, spends another week editing a first cut, then is thanked and dismissed as the Executive Producer takes over the final cut. Some directors shoot multiple episodes, especially on sitcoms (where the director has a bit more clout), while others may only do one or two shows during a season. Whichever, they report to the showrunner on the series.

SELLING SHOWS AND COSTS

The development process is completely different in TV than in the feature world. And unfortunately, as a new writer, it is much harder to sell a new series than it is a feature script, which is not easy in and of itself. Understand, a movie script is a one-shot deal where the buyers know exactly what they're getting. But a TV series is potentially a hundred-episode deal. No one is buying a show simply based on a good pilot script or premise. They need to know what will happen in subsequent episodes, as well as in future seasons. In other words, what they are buying is the writer, and they have to have confidence that that writer can turn out a quality show every week (twenty-two episodes per season for a broadcast network, around fifteen for cable), hopefully for five years. If you don't have a track record of having written for TV before, they have no way of knowing whether you can pull that off. Of course, you can always partner up with an established writer and/or producer, but many of them are looking to develop their own shows. Why share credit and money with a novice? The only way that is going to happen is if you have one heck of an idea.

The average studio movie these days is approaching $100 million. Seems like a lot, right? But an hour TV cop drama can cost $3 million (Netflix and Amazon shows cost even more). Multiply that by twenty-two episodes (fewer for cable and digital) times five years, and the cost of that show could be $330 million. Who pays for all that? Shows are deficit financed, meaning the cost of producing the show is more than the license fee that the network pays to the studio to air it. The production company may put up 25 percent, and the network showing it would pay a broadcast fee of 75 percent. The network will make its money back through commercials (cable channels also get fees from cable provid-

ers, and internet companies get paid directly from sub-
scribers). The higher the ratings of the show, the more the
network can charge its advertisers for a thirty-second spot. The
production company, which owns all the episodes, makes
its money back when it sells the program internationally or,
later on, syndicates the show worldwide. But it needs several
years' worth of episodes to do this. If a show gets canceled
after one season, the production company takes a big hit.
But one successful syndicated show is worth hundreds of
millions of dollars and will pay for a number of shows that
didn't make it.

Keep in mind that today, the production company and
the network are often one and the same. For instance, ABC
Studios (formerly Touchstone Television), which produces
shows, sells many of its series to ABC broadcast network,
but both are owned by the Walt Disney Corporation, which
also owns the Disney Channel, A&E, and ESPN. Universal Television and NBC broadcast network are both owned
by NBC Universal, which also owns Syfy, Bravo, and the
USA Network. It's in the parent corporation's best interest
to keep shows going for as long as possible to recoup costs
in syndication.

SYNDICATION

There are more than 350 local broadcast stations in the
United States. A production company will sell a block of
shows of a particular series to a local station in a certain

market, allowing them a set number of airings over a certain amount of time at a predetermined fee. For instance, the show *Friends* was sold by Warner Bros. Television for $275,000 per cycle, or airing time. Multiply that by all the stations in the country showing reruns of *Friends* on a daily basis and you generate a lot of cash—$950,000,000 in this case, and that was just the first run. If the show performs well, the cycle might then be renewed. The local channels, of course, make their money selling commercial time.

Production companies also sell their shows to cable channels to make even more money. *Seinfeld,* the most successful thirty-minute syndicated show to date, has earned over $3 billion since it went off the air in 1998. And Jerry Seinfeld and Larry David, who own a piece of it, still make tens of millions of dollars each year off of it. (Seinfeld's estimated worth today is over $800 million.) But the key is producing enough episodes to syndicate. Three years is seen as the minimum for a broadcast network show, which translates to sixty-six episodes. But you don't have to be a creator or have an ownership in a show to see money after the initial airing.

TV RESIDUALS

Just like feature films, television shows pay residuals every time an episode airs in rerun, syndication, or internationally. On a network show, all reruns in prime time would pay

100 percent of minimum. On a syndicated show, that percentage drops each time it's shown until the thirteenth airing. From then on, the writer would receive 5 percent of minimum each time. For shows that first aired on basic cable, the second through fifth airings pay 50 percent of minimum, and then it drops steeply to a floor of 1.5 percent for every time the show airs after the twelfth time. Shows that air on foreign television have a slightly different formula.

DEVELOPMENT

The development process for series for the four broadcast networks is seasonal. Usually, a network-approved writer (that ain't you yet) pitches an idea to a production company. If they like it, they make a deal to further develop the idea together and pitch it to a broadcast network, cable channel, or digital outlet. Sometimes, no money is exchanged unless the show can be set up. Other times, they may option an idea or pay for a pilot script to be written. If it is set up, the writer gets a small bonus and writes a pilot script. Pilots pay 150 percent of minimums, though seasoned writers can demand a lot more. If the pilot is produced, the writer would also get a producing credit and a producing fee, which can range from $15,000 to $100,000. If the pilot is picked up by the network, the writer will get a sales bonus, a producing fee for every episode, a fee on each episode for creating the series, plus some kind of profit participation.

Here's the catch—about three hundred ideas for series are pitched to each broadcast network every year between June and November. (Cable and digital outlets do not have this kind of seasonal development.) Of these, only one hundred will get orders for pilot scripts, which will be written from July through December. During this time, you'd work with the production company writing and rewriting the script until you have a kickass first draft. Then the network will read it and give you notes as well. Between January and April, the networks will choose about twenty of these scripts to be shot as pilots. The production companies will usually spend more on the pilot than on a normal episode because they really want it to get picked up. (The *Lost* pilot reportedly cost $12 million.) Then in May, the network will choose around five or six of these produced pilots to be new series come September, plus a couple more as midseason replacements. The exact number will depend on how well the current shows did the previous year. A normal order on a new show would be thirteen episodes out of the twenty-two-episode season. The remainder are called the "back nine" and if the show doesn't get canceled due to low ratings, they are usually ordered up by early December. Networks could also do a short order and only initially ask for six. Of these new series, maybe two or three will get renewed the following May. So you can see, the chances of creating a successful TV series are low. But if you are successful, plan to make many trips to the bank.

STAFFING

After a show is picked up in May, staffing season begins. That's when the Executive Producer (showrunner) hires the writers to work on the show. He will be bombarded by every TV literary agent in town, who'll send him writing samples, trying to get their clients work on the series. Usually, eight to ten writers are eventually hired, and each has one of the various production positions already discussed. Fees are paid weekly and can range from around $4,000 a week for a staff writer to $50,000 a week or more for an Executive Producer. Most of these positions also pay additional money for scripts written and credited. Obviously, ten writers and twenty-two episodes don't amount to many scripts per writer. So what will you be doing in the meantime? Meeting, talking through ideas and future episodes, giving notes on other writers' outlines and scripts, and drinking a lot of coffee.

As a new writer, it is possible to get hired as a staff writer without any prior TV experience if the showrunner wants you working for him. All shows are also required by the WGA to have two freelance scripts written (but not necessarily produced) per season, which opens up the door for getting new people involved in television. In this case, you wouldn't show up to the offices every day and sit in on the meetings, but rather would be told what the episode is about that they want you to write, scene by scene, and you'd turn in the script when done. The only catch with these freelance jobs is that they usually go to friends of the showrunner, other clients of his agent, or destitute relatives needing a job. After all, even if the writer tanks on a twenty-two-minute episode, another writer can fix the script in a week.

ANIMATION

"What's up, doc?" Plenty, if you can create imaginative stories that a talented artist can bring to life on the screen. Today, countless animated feature films, prime-time series, and daytime television shows have flooded both the big screen and small, targeting audiences from preschoolers to adults. Channels such as Cartoon Network, Nickelodeon, Disney Channel, and PBS are full of animated programming for kids, while FOX, Comedy Central, and FX offer more mature fare. And almost every major studio has a constant stream of animated feature films in development. In 2016, six of the top eleven box office films for the year were animated (*Finding Dory, The Secret Life of Pets, Zootopia, The Jungle Book, Sing,* and *Moana*), grossing over $2 billion domestically. Bottom line, the animation industry is a bustling business that's growing every year.

In the feature world, animation scripts are developed in a similar manner to those of live action films. You start with a concept, determine your major plot points, outline the screenplay's three acts, then start writing each scene with full descriptions and dialogue. There are, however, some notable differences between a live action and an animation script. For instance, in live action, you usually leave it up to the director as to how he wants to shoot a particular scene. He'll interpret your words and, along with the cinematographer, choose the camera angles and blocking he thinks work best. But animation is a much more uniquely visual medium than live action. You have to be significantly more specific in your descriptions, telling the director and animators exactly the images you want them to see, shot by shot. For example, in a live action script, you might write:

```
A cat chases a squirrel, up a tree. The feline gets
stuck on a branch, can't get down, and falls off.
```

The director will determine how to shoot this. But in animation, you have to describe exactly what you want the audience to see, including sight gags, facial expressions, props, and locations. The same scene in an animated film or TV show might read as follows:

```
The cat dashes after the squirrel, legs spinning
like bicycle tires, which roll right up the tree
trunk, leaving tracks. The squirrel launches acorns
back at him from out of his mouth like loud machine-
gun fire. The cat comes to a screeching halt atop a
large branch, grabbing leaves to use as a shield.
The squirrel laughs and jumps onto a branch of
an adjacent tree, escaping.

The cat looks down. He is much higher up than he
thought. Staring directly into camera, he gulps.
```

Suddenly, his weight causes the branch to creak and
give way. It snaps, falling down. The cat remains in
the air momentarily, resigned to his fate. The he
plummets downward, leaving his impression in the
turf below.

This is much more of a visual image. And the rule of
thumb is, if you want to see it on-screen, you, as the writer,
had better describe it in sufficient detail for the storyboard
artist to take your words and construct the pictures you have
in mind. This is especially important as many scripts are sent
overseas to be animated. Translation to other languages,
without detailed descriptions, leaves a lot of room for mis-
interpretation. In addition, these added descriptions mean
that an animation script will be a bit longer than a live action script, especially in feature films.

As stated, in live action, the writer is discouraged from
adding camera angles, and instead leaves shot choices to the
director. But in an animated script, you have more freedom
to suggest dramatic or cartoony visuals. If an alarm clock
goes off, you might say it literally bounces on the nightstand.
Or the ringing might jolt a sleeping character right out of
bed onto the floor. Some animation writers prefer to capitalize camera moves, critical images, sound effects, and
music cues to emphasize their importance.

Another distinction between live action and animation
scripts is that the latter are less talky. No one wants to see
cartoon characters simply chatting with little movement on
the screen. And of course, an animated character can do
anything with no budget limitations. Let him land a hot air

balloon full of elephants on the Eiffel Tower, or have him swim among a dozen man-eating sharks, or put him in a spaceship bound for Mars. It's just a drawing and requires no costly special effects. On the other hand, don't put too many characters in one scene as it can be difficult and expensive to draw everyone in and keep them all moving at the same time. Above all, watch a bunch of animated shows to see the little tricks of how things are done.

On the business end, another big difference between animation writing and live action writing is that most animated movies and TV series are *not* under Writers Guild jurisdiction. And no jurisdiction can mean no minimum payments, no residuals, and no health and pension contributions. Years ago, I wrote for a Saturday morning series on FOX called *Life with Louie,* based on the boyhood adventures of comedian Louie Anderson. I got paid $8,000 for each script and that was it, no matter how many times they aired the episode. Now, I'm not complaining. Eight thousand dollars for two weeks' worth of work isn't bad, but it was well below what I would have gotten had it been a live action show. Right now, only FOX prime-time shows, such as *The Simpsons* and *Family Guy,* are covered by the WGA agreement. Other network prime-time shows are negotiated on a case by case basis.

A number of non-prime-time shows are covered, however, by the Animation Guild, an IATSE union that counts around 3,800 animation artists, writers, and technicians as their members. They have a collective bargaining agreement

(CBA) with many companies that produce cartoons, including Cartoon Network, Nickelodeon, and most of the major studios. They have minimum payments, plus health and pension benefits, though separate from the WGA. And while feature films are not covered under Guild jurisdiction, most studios want to hire a WGA writer and agree to minimums (usually more) with benefits so they can get the best talent to pen the scripts. After all, when you're spending tens of millions on a feature-length movie, what's a few thousand dollars more added to the budget?

GRAPHIC NOVELS

Every semester, I find that a few of my screenwriting students are interested in writing graphic novels. For you non-millennials unfamiliar with the term, they are more commonly known as comic books. The difference is that comic books generally come out monthly with a volume and issue number, and run around twenty-two pages with a few more pages for ads. A graphic novel is a one-time storybook that runs much longer, sometimes in the hundreds of pages. It is also printed on better quality paper with a magazine-like binding as opposed to staples.

The reason I will discuss this form of writing in a book about screenwriting is twofold. The first is that graphic novels resemble a script much more than they do a novel. They are visual, have dialogue, and contain normal story structure, complex characters, subplots, and all the other elements of a movie script. The drawings are used to advance the story, in contrast to a regular book with illustrations that are there simply to accompany the text. The second reason is that so many graphic novels are being made into films these days that it is a viable way to break into the movie business, especially if you have artistic talent.

The most important thing to understand, however, is that the best drawings in the world will mean nothing if your story isn't creative, entertaining, and well thought-out. That means coming up with a good premise, developing plot points, generating an outline, and writing the script, all before your colorful pens hit the page. In other words, you need to do all the things you would do if you were writing a normal screenplay.

There are several ways to format a script for a graphic novel. The main thing is to figure out how many panels you want per page, determine what the reader will see in each panel, and create what dialogue the characters in each panel say (or think). A typical script might look like this, though there is no one correct way to format:

PAGE ONE

Panel 1: Tony close-up in car, looks off panel.

Panel 2: A masked man runs down the street past the car.

Panel 3: Tony leaps out of the car after him. The Masked Man glances back, surprised.

TONY: *Hold it right there, my friend!*

MASKED MAN: *No, it can't be!*

Panel 4: The startled Masked Man stops running as Tony gets in his face.

TONY: *Didn't expect to see me again, did ya?*

Panel 5: Tony rips the mask off the man to reveal a shocked Dr. Sinister, who tries to cover his face.

MASKED MAN (DR. SINISTER): *No!!*

Panel 6: Two police cars appear at the end of the alley. Tony smiles.

TONY: *Your days of evil are over, Dr. Sinister.*

Then it'd be on to page 2. Granted, pretty simplistic example, but you get the idea. The main thing you have to remember is to only describe a still picture in each panel, no multiple action. For instance, "Tony races down the street, then takes cover behind the trash bin when the Masked Man pulls out a gun." This wouldn't work because you can't show a character doing more than one action in one panel. The other thing you can include in your script is thumbnails, which are tiny thumb-size drawings made on the script next to each panel representing what the larger, more detailed artwork will look like when the script is put into actual novel form.

There are a few differences between storytelling in screenplays and in graphic novels that you must be aware of. For instance, a graphic novel is less of a collaborative effort. You, as the writer, are the director. You decide what the illustrator will draw and this becomes the final product. In a screenplay, the director interprets your words and shoots the scene as he sees fit. And someone other than you will design the sets and costumes, choose the music, and cast the characters. You must also be careful not to use too many words in a graphic novel for they may crowd out the illustrations, and the point of this medium is to emphasize pictures.

If you're not an artist, you'll need to find one to work with. Unless he's your good friend, it's always best if you can offer some compensation, as this shows your seriousness in the project as well as your professionalism. Once the project is completed, you can submit your work to publishers and agents, or self-publish. Putting the book on a website that people can access (even if with a password) is a good way to display your work. In addition, you should attend comic book conventions. There are many across the country going on weekly and they feature writers, artists, dealers, workshops, films, exhibits, and more. Most are fairly inexpensive to attend and you might want to pay for a booth so that attendees can visit you and see your offerings. Never know when you'll make a good connection.

Studios are interested in turning graphic novels into films now more than ever before. Dozens, including *Watchmen, 300,* and *Road to Perdition,* have already been made, along with those based on the many DC and Marvel comics characters, such as X-Men, Batman, Wolverine, Superman, Captain America, and Thor. (Disney even bought Marvel for $4 billion several years ago.) More are on the way. They generally attract a large audience of young males who like action movies, and can turn into franchise films, spawning sequel after sequel and adding big box office numbers to a studio's tally.

VIDEO GAMES

Breathing, eating, sleeping, and gaming—better known to some people as the four necessities of life. While movies and television may be two of the most favorite forms of entertainment today, neither can compete with the massive popularity (and in some cases, obsession) of video games. What started in the early 1970s with a simplistic diversion called *Pong* quickly expanded into a lucrative business when *Pac-Man, Donkey Kong,* and *Space Invaders* hit the market. Now, decades later, gaming has become a $100 billion a year global industry, if one accounts for the sales of console hardware and software; online, mobile, and PC games; as well as social networking games. That's almost triple what the $35 billion worldwide box office was for movies in 2016 (though this figure does not include DVD or TV sales, nor other ancillary markets). In fact, gaming has become so prevalent in our society that some colleges now offer degrees in video game design. And every year, the Writers Guild of America gives out an award for Outstanding Achievement in Videogame Writing (though the producers who get nominated must be signatories of the Guild).

Don't think, however, that it's fanatical young boys who are causing the video game business to flourish. The average age of a gamer is thirty-five, and 44 percent are women while 25 percent are over the age of fifty. In addition, the gaming industry employs over 200,000 people in the United States alone, which includes designers, computer programmers, animators and artists, translators, testers, marketers, tech support, sales crews, and of course, writers. Every year, hundreds of new titles are released from large and small companies alike to go with the most popular ones of today, which include *Call of Duty, Madden NFL, Grand Theft Auto, Skylanders, Minecraft,* and many multiplayer games.

Writing video games is both similar to and different than writing a movie script. Both require a narrative and many video games also have dialogue. However, creating a video game is much more of a collaborative effort. The writer must work with a designer to discuss story, characters, set pieces and settings, and how it all fits in with the game's mechanics and levels. Gameplay must always come first, and it must be integrated seamlessly into the narrative. But before a writer gets into all these details with the designer, he first needs a basic story. Sometimes it's the writer who comes up with an original premise, and other times the story is conceived before the writer is brought in, especially when the idea is based on a popular movie or a spin-off of an existing game. (Nowadays, successful video games are also being developed into movies, as in *Minecraft: The Movie* from War-ner Bros.)

If you're creating an original game, the first thing you must do is write an overview of your story. This should tell everything that happens from the opening scene of the game, through the major steps, and all the way to the game's completion. Is it a real-time strategy game (RTS) where players gather resources, attack other players, and gameplay occurs at the same time for everyone as opposed to "by turn"? Or is it a role-playing game (RPG) where players create their own characters, based on certain skills and traits, and then go on a long adventure made up of shorter quests? Is it a linear plot where the player simply needs to beat each level to move on, or does it have multiple branching plots? Who is the protagonist and antagonist? What are the obstacles? This overview should be written in prose and be several pages long. It is the sales tool you will send to companies to see if they might be interested in developing your project.

If accepted, you would then work with the designer and elaborate further on the world you have created, including the locations and levels, and what it all should look like. Then you would construct a flowchart for your game, ex-plaining the many decisions a player will have to make and how each opens up a whole new path for that player to take. These interactions are critical to the story and take the player on very different paths toward the game's conclusion. The flowchart should consist of text boxes with arrows to indi-cate what happens when various actions are performed. In addition, you should create side quests and explain each one of these as well.

A writer must also generate detailed character descriptions and bios, along with all of the relationships for all the major characters in the game. This includes the player character (PC), the one you control in the game, as well as for the non-player characters (NPC) who will pop up time and time again and interact with the PC. Include personality details, physical descriptions, and backstories for everyone and everything important to the main story of the world. Dialogue needs to be written as well, assuming your game has speaking parts. You progress through each scene of your story and detail all the necessary information. Write out interactions with NPCs using flowcharts showing how they respond to what you say, do, or give to them. You should also flowchart any puzzles, mazes, or quests the player faces.

Then you'll need to write cut scenes, which are short non-interactive animations or movies that come before or after major plot points in your story that break up gameplay. They can be used to show conversations between characters, reward the player for achieving a major milestone, create emotional connections, or foreshadow future events, but should always be written to enhance or describe the story. Then write the actual storyboard script, which is quite detailed and similar to a movie script.

There are several different formats for scripts, but be consistent. Include dialogue, camera angles, what the player sees, what decisions he has to make, and what the programmers need to know. This will include any important rooms, objects, or NPCs that will be encountered in each episode. You can also include notes on music played, sound effects, or environmental effects. For example, if you want it to rain at a certain point, blinding the player, include that detail.

When writing a video game script you have to remember that you're doing this not for the game player, but for the game developer who has the means to bring your concept to fruition. He needs a complete picture of what your game is about, so you must create a world complete with a tone, sounds, characters, story, plot, and subplots. This means your script must have far more detail than a normal movie script to allow one to see all the creative possibilities.

There are numerous books that have been written recently that discuss the ins and outs of writing video games in elaborate detail. If this is an area that interests you, I recommend reading some of them to find out a lot more information on the subject. There is also video game writing software available to help with your script and flowcharts. In addition, you should attend conferences, meet with game writers, and follow them on social media, asking relevant questions. When it comes to video games, the future is now.

GLOSSARY OF TERMS

You've got to know what you're talking about when conversing with a producer or executive. When I first got started, I met with an older producer who asked me if the story I was telling him was a "broad" comedy. I had no idea what that meant and assumed he was referring to an archaic, unflattering term for a woman. Since my leads were both men, I told him, "Not at all," then proceeded to pitch him the silliest broad comedy this side of *Dumb and Dumber*. Boy, did I feel stupid afterward. Here are some terms you should know about before taking your first meeting.

Above-the-Line Costs: Portion of the budget that covers major creative participants (writer, director, actors, and producer) including script and story development costs. The phrase comes from the budget top sheet, which separates above- and below-the-line costs with—what else?—a line. With top actors getting $20 million a pop, it's one of the main reasons studio movies cost so much.

Adaptation: A script based on previously existing written or filmed material, such as a book, a TV show, a prior movie, or a play. Studios make more adapted films today than original projects due to the lower risk of an established audience and built-in marketing. A lot of good that does a new writer with his first spec, huh?

Agent Trainee: A person starting work at a talent agency, learning the tools and techniques required to eventually become an agent. It's a lot of menial work for little money, but it's a foot in the door.

Alan Smithee: A once-clandestine pseudonym that the Directors Guild of America used to allow directors to use when they wished to remove their name from a film they were embarrassed to be a part of. It worked fine until the movie *An Alan Smithee Film* came out in the late '90s, and the cat was out of the bag.

Ancillary Rights: Contractual agreements in which revenue is derived from subsidiary income sources beyond the theatrical release of a film. These include sales of action figures, posters, CDs, books, TV shows, T-shirts, etc. Years ago these amounted to very little. Today they often account for more than the original domestic ticket receipts. Fox will forever regret giving George Lucas all merchandising rights to *Star Wars,* a movie they had little confidence in back in 1977.

Answer Print: The first composite (sound and picture) motion picture print from the laboratory with editing, score, and mixing completed. Usually color values, which are a numerical figure signifying the intensity of a color's components, will need to be corrected before a release print is made.

Anti-hero: The main protagonist of a film who lacks the characteristics of your typically admired all-American hero. In other words, girls, the guy you better not bring home to meet daddy. Think Jeff Lebowski, Dirty Harry, Jack Sparrow, or TV's Walter White.

Art House Film: Usually a classy low-budget film with some sort of artistic merit, shown in a smaller theater. These include foreign-language films and movies about subject matter that would not appeal to a mass audience. They don't generally clean up at the box office.

Assistant Director (AD): An aide to the director in the filmmaking process who helps in the organization and shooting of specific scenes. It's a union position and should not be confused with a Director's Assistant, who's the person who fetches the boss's dry cleaning and drops his kids off at school.

Associate Producer: Although this credit alludes to a variety of things, the associate producer usually acts as a supporting producer and sometimes has little to do with the movie other than passing the script along to someone who does. It's the lowest-level producer credit on a film.

Auteur: A French term that revolves around the theory that the director is the true creator, or author, of a film, and is the one whose vision we see on screen. Naturally, writers vehemently disagree, as filmmaking is a collaborative effort and the director is only one of the contributors.

Automated Dialogue Replacement (ADR or Looping): The rerecording of dialogue by actors in a sound studio during postproduction, usually performed to playback of edited picture in order to match lip movements on screen. It's frequently used to replace tracks of poor quality (e.g., due to high levels of background noise) or to change the delivery or inflection of a line, particularly when the actor plain and simply stinks.

Back End: Profit participation in a film after distribution and/or production costs have been recouped. Unless you're a big star, producer, or director, it's imaginary money.

Based on a True Story: A Hollywood marketing ploy to get an audience to think the events in a movie are the way things actually happened. In truth, this phrase gives the creators a vast license to change just about everything for dramatic effect.

Below-the-Line Costs: The technical expenses and labor involved in the actual making of a movie, including set construction, crew, camera equipment, film stock, developing, and printing. On a low-budget indie film, above-the-line is cheap. This is your real expense.

Billing: The relative sizes, positions, and order of credits on screen and in advertising. A person whose name is shown first in the credits or whose name is at the top of an ad or poster has gotten "top billing." If two names appears at the same time or at the same height, they are said to have "equal billing."

Blind Bidding: When theater owners have to bid on a movie without seeing it, usually because it is not yet finished.

Blockbuster: A movie that makes a ton of moolah at the box office. It used to mean any film that passed $100 million upon domestic release, but nowadays that's almost expected. *Jaws* is considered the first blockbuster, based on how many people lined up to see it back in 1975, though there were earlier films that actually made more money.

Blow-Up: Optical process of enlarging a film, usually from 16mm to 35mm.

Bomb: A movie which is a financial disaster. Some of the classic ones include *Heaven's Gate* (1980), *Ben-Hur* (2016), *Waterworld* (1995), *Gigli* (2003), and *John Carter* (2012). Some of these films actually made a lot of money, but cost a whole lot more.

Bootleg: An unofficial and illegal copy of a movie, often of a substandard quality, sometimes made from a hidden video camera in a theater showing the movie. You used to be able to buy them openly on the streets of Seventh Avenue in Manhattan. Not so much anymore.

Box Office Receipts: What the theater owner takes in from ticket sales to customers at the box office. A portion of this revenue, called film rental, is remitted to the studio/distributor in the form of rental payments. It can be up to 90 percent on a popular movie, though the split may change downward every week.

Break: To open a film in several theaters simultaneously, either in and around a single city or in a group of cities, or on a national basis. Some movies open in twenty theaters, others three thousand.

Breakout: To expand bookings after an initial period of exclusive or limited engagement.

Buzz: A film that's getting good word of mouth.

Cameo: A bit part played by a famous actor who would ordinarily not take such a small part, but does so because he's friends with the director, it's a high-profile project, or he owes someone a favor. Usually it's uncredited and surprises the audience when the actor first appears.

CGI (Computer-Generated Imagery): The use of computer graphics to create or enhance special effects. They can do practically anything these days, but it ain't cheap.

Character Actor: An actor who specializes in playing a particular style of character, often stereotypical, offbeat, or humorous. You know their face, but not always their name.

Chick Flick: Movies that appeal to women, often with a female lead, and are usually emotional and a bit sappy. A good date film, but the guy may hate it.

Cinematographer: Also known as Director of Photography (DP). He's responsible for elements viewed through the lens and works closely with the director to create appropriate shots and organize the visual elements of a scene, including the selection of film stock, cameras and lenses, and lighting. A good one can enhance the film; a bad one can destroy it.

Cinema Verité: A type of filmmaking that uses documentary-style shooting and is usually done with simple cameras and equipment.

Completion Bond: A kind of insurance that guarantees the film will be completed on time and on budget, or pays the cost in the event that the producer exceeds the budget. They are usually for independent films (as studios self-insure) and are required by banks and investors before they'll hand over any money. If invoked, the completion guarantor takes over the production and recoups its money before any other investors.

Concept: It's what your movie is about. The premise. The idea. What happens to your main character. A good logline may define it.

Continuity: How consistent is your movie? Is your lead actor's necktie tight in one angle, and loose in another angle of the same scene? That's bad continuity. Every movie has some inconsistent continuity and it's fun to see if you can pick it out.

Co-Producer: A position less than a producer but more than an associate producer. He usually has a certain responsibility for the development and/or production of the movie.

Cross Collateralization: A method by which distributors offset financial losses in one area or market against revenue derived from others. For example, if an actor has a two-picture deal with a studio and the first movie loses money, they may deduct those losses against his second film. If so, everyone with profit participation on the second film gets screwed.

Crossover Film: A film that is targeted to a certain demographic but finds an audience in a much wider market. If your movie made $500 million at the box office, it was probably a crossover film.

Dailies: As the film is shot, production personnel and studio executives view raw, unedited footage the following day. This footage is known as dailies, or rushes. If things don't look right, or the production is behind schedule, the director may be on the hot seat and, on rare occasion, immediately replaced.

Day-for-Night: A shoot done during that day that simulates nighttime, using filters, underexposure, and other techniques to create a feeling of darkness. Sometimes there's no way to avoid this because of scene scheduling.

Deal Memo: A letter or short contract that spells out the major terms of an agreement before the much longer contract is finalized. A deal memo allows the writer to get paid and to start writing, since it could be months before the actual contract is ready to be signed.

Deferment: When writers, directors, cast, crew, or others accept postponing a portion of their compensation until first profits in order to reduce production costs. This is more common with low-budget independent films where people reduce their normal fees in order to make the budget work than it is in studio projects. If a finished movie does not earn profits, the deferred payment holders will not be paid their deferred fee, and even it if does, they may only see a fraction of it.

Development: The process of taking a story from idea to green-lit script. Along the way, a writer may work with a producer, studio executive, director, or actor to mold the script into its final product and get talent attached. When this process goes on for years, the project is known to be in "development hell."

Development Executive: The person at the studio whose job it is to develop all those screenplays that never get made. D-people find material, give notes on scripts, meet with new writers and directors, and push their projects along. Their titles may be vice president, director, manager, or story editor.

Director's Cut: The director is required by the Directors Guild of America (DGA) to be allowed to edit the first version of the film they've just shot, known as the director's cut. After that, the studio that hired them can allow them to continue, or take over the project. Top-name directors like Spielberg, Cameron, and Scorsese usually have final cut approval.

Distributor: They are responsible for marketing a film, which includes release dates, promotion and advertising, bookings into theaters, and DVD and TV sales. The distributor and production company can be subsidiaries of the same corporation, as with the major studios, or separate entities.

A film that can't find a distributor is like a novel without a publisher. It probably won't be seen by many.

Domestic Rights: Usually defined as the United States and English-speaking Canada. Everywhere else is foreign.

Editor: This is the person who cuts the film, nowadays using an Avid and/or digital splicing mechanisms. His or her work starts after the first day of shooting and continues until the final cut.

Elements: This is how you turn your script into gold. Elements are the people who get attached to your script (i.e., director, actors, and/or producers), whose involvement increases the value of your script and makes it more likely that a studio will buy and greenlight the project. Beware, however—the wrong elements can kill a deal as well.

Ensemble: A film with a large cast, none of whom has a true lead. There are usually multiple interwoven plotlines that connect the characters. Examples include *Pulp Fiction, The Breakfast Club,* and *Nashville.*

Execute: To complete, to sign, to perform. It's what you do to your contract.

Executive Producer: A high-ranking credited person who is generally not involved with the actual day-to-day making of the movie. On an indie film, he may be the person who raises the money. On a studio film, he may simply be the manager of one of the stars.

Exhibitor: These are the movie theaters that show the films. Most of their income comes from the popcorn, candy, and soft drinks they sell, hence the outrageous concession prices.

Exposition: Background information necessary to tell the audience so they understand the story better. A good writer tries to insert this organically within the context of the film.

Extra: A person who appears in a movie, but as part of a crowd or in the background of a scene, like at a ballgame or walking on a city street. Though they don't have speaking lines and Hollywood does not consider them to be actors, they do get paid for their "performance," sometimes a hundred bucks a day, along with a crappy lunch.

Fast Track: A project in development that the studio really wants to make . . . and soon. Sometimes it's so it can be released by a certain date, other times to beat another studio that's developing a similar script to the theater.

Feature Film: A full-length movie, generally between 90 and 120 minutes long, that usually includes a basic three-act story structure, character arcs, and multiple settings. Roughly six hundred movies were released in America last year, but many saw limited release in just a few theaters, looking for a broader distribution deal.

Festival: An event that showcases films, some from amateurs, some from professionals, vying for awards and prizes. The big ones are Sundance, Toronto, Venice, Berlin, SXSW, Tribeca, and Cannes, but there are literally hundreds worldwide. Win one and there's a reasonable chance your movie might find a distributor.

Film Buyer: A go-between who arranges to buy films from a distributor on behalf of an exhibitor.

Film Noir: A French phrase coined in the early 1940s that refers to a genre of sexy, stylized crime dramas. Examples include *The Big Sleep, Chinatown, Taxi Driver,* and *Pulp Fiction.*

Film Rental: The money that a theater owner pays the distributor for the right to show the movie. This can be anywhere from 30 to 90 percent of the box office (less his expenses), depending on the anticipated popularity of the film. The percentage drops the longer the movie is out. Remember, the theater owner wants to fill as many seats as possible, for his money is mostly made at the concession stand.

Final Cut: This is what the movie will look like in the theater. Most studios or financiers of a picture retain final cut. Only the A-list directors can demand this.

Financier: This is the money guy. He doesn't develop the script but comes up with the funding for packaged products ready to be shot.

First-Dollar Gross: The best type of profit participation for talent, in which their cut is determined before studio accounting whittles down the profits. Only big-time movie stars, directors, and producers get this in their deal.

First-Look Deal: When a writer or producer accepts money from a studio, and in exchange the studio has first right of refusal on any projects he writes or develops.

First Run: The first time a new film is shown in the theaters.

Fish Out of Water: A type of movie, usually a comedy, in which the main character is thrown into an unfamiliar place or situation and must figure out how to survive. *Sleeper, Beverly Hills Cop,* and *Back to the Future* are good examples.

Floors: The minimum percentage of box office receipts a distributor is entitled to receive no matter what the theater's operating expenses may be. Like film rentals, they also decline week by week, and are generally in the 25 to 70 percent range.

Foley: The art of re-creating sound effects, like running up steps, in sync with the visuals of a movie. The sounds are often exaggerated for effect and accomplished in unusual means, such as slapping celery stalks against a wooden chair to re-create fistfight noises.

Foreign Sales: Any film licensed outside the United States and Canada is considered a foreign sale. Today, the foreign box office is usually larger than the domestic box office on most films.

Fourth Wall: The imaginary wall that separates the character's on-screen world from the real world of the audience watching them. When the character looks straight into the camera and talks directly to the audience, sometimes as an aside, he is said to have "broken" the fourth wall.

Four-Walling: This is when a studio or producer rents a theater and its staff for a set price, usually to screen the movie to employees, guests, or potential distributors. If there's any box office involved, the renter keeps it all and the exhibitor simply keeps his flat fee.

Franchise Film: The lifeblood of the major studios. These are movies that live on and on, sequel after sequel, and make hundreds of millions for the company along with a nice paycheck for all the talent involved. Some of the more successful ones have been *Star Wars, The Fast and the Furious, Pirates of the Caribbean, Harry Potter, Rocky, Indiana Jones,* and anything that started out as a

Marvel comic. This is why studios shy away from original fare.

F**k You Money: This is when you've made so much coinage over the years, you can live the luxurious lifestyle you desire without ever working again and don't care about insulting, offending, or disparaging those who disagree with your brilliant ideas, or don't like your pet projects.

Going Over People's Heads: When you're not happy with one person's decision, you contact the person above them. A dangerous thing to do unless you have plenty of clout in the industry (see F**k You Money). Generally, once an executive at a company turns down your project, it's dead at that place unless new elements become attached. That's why you have to choose carefully which person you send your script to.

Greenlight: When a project gets a greenlight it means the production company has decided to make the movie and preproduction will soon begin. The script should be ready to shoot, and cast and crew are assembled. But as a writer, don't spend your bonus check yet. That is paid the first day of shooting, and many a project has fallen apart before then.

Green Screen: A type of special effect in which a scene is shot on a soundstage in front of a green screen, and an image is later superimposed as a background. Think Superman flying between high-rise buildings. It used to be a blue screen, but it seems green works better.

Gross Receipts: A studio or distributor's revenues derived from all sales, including film rentals, television, DVDs, merchandising, and any other ancillary markets.

Guerrilla Film: A low-budget indie film, usually shot on the fly without any location permits, union workers, elaborate props, or even professional talent. Don't let the cops catch you shooting.

High Concept: A script or story that possesses a great marketing hook and allows the audience to immediately know what the movie is all about. With a high-concept idea, your logline should jump off the page.

Hip Pocket: In the writing world, this is when an agent agrees to represent one particular script of yours without signing you on as a full-time client, due to time limitations or uncertainty about the material. If the script sells, he'll sign you. If not, hasta la vista, baby.

Hot: Anyone whose last picture was a big hit, won an Academy Award, and is being pursued by every agent, producer, and studio executive in town . . . at least for a week or two until someone else even hotter comes along.

Housekeeping Deal: When a studio supplies talent with offices, assistants, and overhead expenses in exchange for first crack at whatever they are writing or developing.

Hyphenates: People who take on more than one major role on a movie, such as producer-director, writer-director, actor-director, or even actor-writer-producer-director. Great if you've got a big ego.

Idea: Every movie began with an idea. An original idea comes directly from the creator's mind. An adaptation takes an existing idea, such as an older movie, TV show, or novel, and expands on it or takes it in a new direction (or sometimes, simply repeats the original idea ad nauseam).

Independent Producer: Producers who work outside the studio system. They develop their own projects, secure their own financing for films, and then seek distribution. Unlike studio movies, these films are usually lower-budget original projects and often sweep the accolades during awards season.

Industry Friends: People you know in the business. The more you know, the more opportunities there are for you to work. If you're lucky, they may even like you.

Legs: A movie that keeps returning a nice box office week after week after week.

Line Producer: The hands-on guy in charge of a film set who organizes all the necessary aspects of production, including budgeting and scheduling. Though he may be the most important guy on the set, next to the director, his credit is usually at the end of the film.

Location Manager: The person who finds the many different places needed to shoot the movie, and then arranges the permits, fees, and legal issues to make it all happen.

MacGuffin: A term popularized by Alfred Hitchcock. It refers to information that a character considers important, or an object he or she may be trying to obtain, but ultimately has no bearing on what the film is really about. For example, Orson Welles's character's dying word in *Citizen Kane* was "Rosebud," but the movie was simply about his life. The same with the old lady's necklace in *Titanic*. It gets the story going but is not the focus of the movie.

Majors: Another name for the big Hollywood movie studios: 20th Century Fox, Sony Pictures, Warner Bros., Paramount Pictures, Universal, and Disney—all owned by even bigger corporations.

Manager: A talent or literary representative who gets more involved in a client's long-term career than an agent. Many also attach themselves as producers to their clients' projects and take a producing fee as opposed to a commission.

Master: The final edited and completed film, ready to be copied and distributed.

Merchandising Rights: The right to license, manufacture, and distribute merchandise based on characters, places, or events in a motion picture. These can be T-shirts, action figures, lunchboxes, toys, etc. An especially lucrative arena for children's movies.

Mini-Multiple: Type of release in select theaters which is bigger than a limited release (twenty venues) but less than a wide release (three thousand venues). Usually, a wider break comes later.

Mockumentary: A fictional, comedic film that is shot to look like a documentary, but makes fun of its subject matter. Example would be *This Is Spinal Tap, Waiting for Guffman,* and *Drop Dead Gorgeous.*

MPAA: An acronym for Motion Picture Association of America, the organization that represents the interests of the major motion picture studios, best known to the public as the governing body that rates every picture G, PG, PG-13, R, or NC-17.

Multi-Tiered Audience: An audience of different demographics who are drawn to a film for different reasons. Different types of marketing must be deployed to reach them all.

Negative Cost: Actual cost of making a movie, but not marketing it. In addition to production costs, it includes overhead, interest, and other expenses, which increase what it really costs to make, and affects profit participation.

Negative Pickup: A distributor guarantees distribution rights to a production company upon completion of their film. The production company can then use this guarantee to help raise money to make the movie.

Net Profits: A contractually defined term that really has nothing to do with whether the movie made more money than it cost, and everything to do with the ways studios can take certain fees from the revenue, exclude certain things from the calculation of revenue, and tack on exorbitant interest rates to make sure it is impossible for you to ever see a dime. Writers always get 5 percent of net profits on paper, but I've never met one who's bolstered his bank account yet.

Networking: Otherwise known as schmoozing, it involves building personal relationships around your business contacts, which increase your chances of continually working in the industry.

Novelization: A book adapted from a motion picture. Or sometimes, a book adapted from a motion picture, which was originally adapted from a book.

Obtaining Rights: A legal means of owning a piece of intellectual property, whether it be a book, story, or someone's personal experience.

One Sheet: The movie poster, usually highly artistic, containing all the main credits of the film.

On Spec: Writing a script on your own for no money in hopes that you will be able to sell it one day. If not, it will hopefully serve as a good writing sample.

Open: The time that a movie is first released in theaters. They often open at different times in different regions of the country as well as internationally.

Open Assignment: Movie projects a studio or production company have that are in search of a writer. Could be a producer's idea, an adaptation, or a rewrite of another writer.

Option: The right to acquire ownership of an intellectual property for a predetermined amount of time. During that time, the buyer often attempts to package together other elements of the film. If a buyer exercises their option to acquire the rights within the designated time, they pay the remainder of purchase costs.

Original Material: Not derived or adapted from another work.

Outline: A document that lists the major scenes within each act of the story. Most movies have around fifty-five scenes in total.

Outtake: A scene that is shot but ultimately not used in a movie. The funny ones become bloopers and are sometimes shown over closing credits.

P&A: Prints and advertising. These are the major costs of film distribution and marketing. Most films are distributed digitally nowadays, as opposed to costly prints.

Packaging: Combining elements such as a director, actors, and a writer to a project before submitting it to a studio in order to increase its value. Large agencies package scripts all the time. The downside for a writer is that if the wrong elements are attached, it can hurt a project as well.

Pay or Play: A phrase used in Hollywood that means a writer (or other talent) is guaranteed his fee, even if the studio changes its mind and doesn't have the script written or, once written, decides not to make the movie. Pay or play does not apply if you are unable to meet your obligations due to fault of your own, such as jail time, rehab stay, or fleeing the country.

Pickups: Movies made by one company that have been acquired by another. It can also refer to footage shot after production wraps.

Pitch: A meeting where a writer tells his movie idea in detail to a producer or executive in hopes of getting hired to write the screenplay. They don't sell as easily as they once did.

Postproduction: Once principal photography had ended, postproduction begins. This is when all the raw footage is edited, sound effects and music are added, computer graphics are inserted, and reshoots are done. Postproduction can sometimes save or kill a project.

Premiere: The first official screening of a movie. Usually a red-carpeted, star-studded affair in New York or LA, attended by the movie's stars, the media, and other celebrities. A glitzy party generally follows. Credited writers are required to be invited pursuant to the WGA MBA.

Preproduction: Once a movie is greenlit, the producers and director assemble the key personnel of the movie. Budgets are made, schedules created, locations scouted, costumes picked out, and the crew hired.

Prequel: A movie, based on another movie, that presents the story and characters *before* the setting of the previously released film. Examples are *Star Wars: Episodes I, II, III*.

Principal Photography: The filming of the main portion of a motion picture involving the lead actors.

Print: A projectable version of a movie, usually consisting of several reels. Each print sent to a theater costs the distributor a couple thousand dollars, so a wide release in three thousand theaters adds up to a pretty penny. That's why studios prefer to distribute their films digitally, as the costs are nominal. A theater, however, must have a digital projector for this, and these can cost upward of a hundred thousand dollars each.

Producer: Different meanings on different films, but generally he or she is the one in charge of the entire production from preproduction through postproduction, and has the most power other than the director.

Production Assistant: A low-level person responsible for various odd jobs on the set. This may include delivering scripts, running errands, light office work, fetching the director his favorite type of doughnut, etc.

Production Company: The entity that makes the movie. They develop the script, hire the talent and crew, and find the financing to shoot the film.

Production Executive: A person who works for a production company. Their job is to find material, develop it, package it, and take it to a financier for funding.

Production Manager: A high-level crew position involved with preproduction and principal photography.

He helps coordinate scheduling, budgeting, and script breakdown.

Purchase Agreement: In film, it's a legal agreement that states the transfer of rights from one company to another. These rights include areas such as television, video, merchandising, foreign sales, etc.

Quote: The amount a writer got paid on his last project, which will determine how much he makes on his next.

Red Herring: A storytelling device where a plot point or event is deliberately set up to make viewers think one thing is going to happen, but it turns out to be irrelevant, or the opposite happens. For example, in *The Bodyguard,* a crazed fan appears to be the singer's stalker, but it turns out the real guy chasing her is a hired assassin.

Release: When a movie is sent to the theaters for audience viewing.

Remake: A new production of a previously produced film. Otherwise known as business as usual in Hollywood.

Rights: What the owner of a specific film grants to a buyer for a fee that allows them to distribute the product for profit in different mediums, such as foreign, television, cable, etc.

Rough Cut: An early assemblage of footage of the film, often significantly longer than the final release.

Run: The length of time a movie plays in theaters, generally calculated in weeks.

Running Time: The length of the movie from start to finish, usually between 90 and 120 minutes for a feature film.

Scale: The minimum amount a writer, director, or actor can be paid on a union project, as determined by the agreement negotiated between their guild and the studios.

Screening: The showing of a movie, typically at a theater. Can also refer to a private showing by the distributor for people associated with the film.

Script Supervisor: The person who tracks which parts of a movie have been filmed and how the filmed scenes differ from the script. They also make continuity notes.

Second Unit: A small, subordinate crew responsible for filming less important shots, such as inserts, crowds, scenery, etc.

Sequel: A film whose story occurs after the original movie took place. It usually features the same characters and actors. At least for the first sequel.

Shooting Schedule: Tells the principals and crew what will be shot on which particular days, and the times people need to be on the set.

Shooting Script: The last version of the script used for production purposes. Each scene is numbered to identify what will be shot and when.

Sides: Specific pages of a script given to an actor to read during an audition.

Sleeper: A movie that becomes an unexpected hit and stays in the theaters for longer than originally anticipated.

Soundstage: A huge building (usually on a studio lot) where intricate sets are built to look like an actual setting. They allow the production to control sound, lighting, weather, and security much better than a real location.

Spoiler: Information about the story or ending of a movie that ruins the suspense or fun of other viewers if they have this knowledge in advance. When discussing this type of info, people often warn their listeners with a "spoiler alert," giving them plenty of time to clear the area. For example, Bruce Willis's character is dead all along in *The Sixth Sense*. That's a spoiler. Hope you've already seen the movie.

Story Analyst or Reader: A person who works for a studio, a producer, or independently, and reads submitted scripts for evaluation. They are often one of the lowest-level people at the company, and may not know a great deal about filmmaking. Then again, their bosses sometimes know even less.

Storyboard: Drawings of scenes from a script to help the director and cinematographer visualize what will be shot. It's usually for action sequences.

Story Conference: A meeting attended by the writer, producers, executives, and director (if on board), where the writer receives suggestions on how to improve his script. If the suggestions are not implemented to the others' satisfaction, the next story conference is usually with a new writer.

Story Editor: Similar to a story analyst or reader, but higher up on the production company's totem pole of who's who. They advise on submitted material and report to a higher-level executive.

Studio Executive: A person who works for a studio, as opposed to simply a production company, and has the power to buy ideas, develop scripts, and help decide which projects to finance and turn into movies.

Submission Release Form: A legal document signed by a writer and producer when submitting a script that is not represented by a literary agent or lawyer. It is used to protect the recipient of the material from liability regarding intellectual property. Most companies require this form on unsolicited submissions.

Syndication: The sale of a film or television show to independent commercial television stations and cable channels in different regions of the country. This is when the big money rolls in.

Talent: A general term for actors, directors, and writers, though some talent agencies only represent actors. Attaching talent to your script can make it a lot more desirable to a buyer. However, not all talent has talent, so be careful who is attached.

Tentpole: A buzzword for a film that is expected to do well at the box office, make a bundle in ancillary markets, and become a franchise for a studio. They usually get a wide release and lots of promotion.

Tracking: Inside sources that allow industry professionals to keep track of what scripts are being submitted, what is selling, which writers are getting jobs, what elements are attached to a script, etc. Some tracking boards can be accessed online through paid subscription.

Trades: The daily and weekly newspapers of the industry, namely *Variety* and *The Hollywood Reporter*, that cover all facets of the entertainment world.

Trailer: A short advertisement for an upcoming movie which contains scenes from the film. They're usually shown before another film appearing in the theater.

Translation: Reproducing a film from one language into another.

Treatment: A five- to ten-page synopsis of your entire movie, written in simple prose, usually before the script is started. If financed independently, the treatment may be used as part of the initial fundraising package.

Turnaround: When a studio decides it's not going to make a movie, the screenplay can be taken to another studio, provided the new studio pays back the costs incurred by the first studio. Since only a small fraction of scripts developed actually get made into movies, pretty much everything goes into turnaround, and studios sometimes horse-trade projects and negotiate over which costs get paid and which get written off.

Unit Publicist: A member of the publicity department who works on location during the production of a movie. Duties include distributing press kits to the media, setting up interviews with actors, and getting word out about the film.

Unsolicited Submissions: Submissions of scripts from writers not represented or not known to the producer or executive. Most professional companies will not consider unsolicited material because of possible legal ramifications and reader time constraints.

Wide Release: The release of a film in numerous theaters, usually between eight hundred and five thousand.

Window: Period of time in which a film is available in a given medium. Windows may be open ended, such as theatrical and home video, or limited, such as pay television or syndication.

Work-for-Hire: A script that a writer is hired to write by a production company, under terms agreed to by both parties.

Working Title: The name by which a movie is known while it is being made. This is sometimes different from the title with which it is released. For instance, *Casablanca* was known by its original stage play name, *Everybody Comes to Rick's*. *Alien* was *Star Beast*. *Pulp Fiction* was *Black Mask*.

Workprint: A print of a picture used only for editing purposes so as to protect the original print from any damage.

LOOKS LIKE YOU MADE IT

Great, you've made it to the end of this book. Now you know everything about the creative and business sides of writing movies. Go finish that script, submit it to buyers, and make millions. You're ready to compete with the big boys and girls.

Uh, not so fast.

In truth, the best advice I can still give you is to abandon your dream of becoming a professional screenwriter and pursue a career with a much more promising future, such as computer programmer, civil engineer, or kindergarten teacher. Don't have a college degree? Become an electrician, or a plumber, or a paralegal. Anything that offers a little security and a steady paycheck. Struggling for success and facing countless rejection for years and years is no way to live life.

But we both know you're not going to do that.

HECK NO!!! There's a writer inside you with stories that need to be told, and you're going to pursue your creative desires until somebody, somehow, somewhere recognizes that and helps you reach your goals. No agent, producer, manager, studio executive (or screenwriting book author) is going to convince you that your dream is a foolish one. You know that hundreds of new writers break into the entertainment business every year, and one of these years it's going to be you. And whether you make it big or not, you will never look back and regret not trying.

At what point will you consider yourself a success? When will you know that you have really made it in the movie business? That differs for every writer. For me, success has always been about enjoying each individual step of the journey. Signing with your first agent . . . optioning your first screenplay . . . selling your first studio project . . . getting your first film made. These are all defining moments in a writer's career. But so are the little things, like the first time you walk around a studio backlot . . . or meet a movie star . . . or are taken to lunch at a posh restaurant . . . or use your earnings to buy your first house. The downside of success is that no matter how well you do, there is always more success to be had, so the quest for absolute success is, in truth, unattainable. But perhaps I am getting a bit philosophical. Enjoying what you do and getting paid to do it is what every writer strives for, and you don't need to win any awards or write any blockbuster movies to achieve that.

There's an old joke about a New York tourist who asks a man who's walking down the street, "How do I get to Carnegie Hall?" The response he gets is, "Practice, practice, practice." That's what you need to do as well. Only write,

write, write. And don't be discouraged if your first script turns out to be nothing more than a painful learning experience that you never submit to anyone. Keep at it and you will get better. And with a little talent, a knowledge of the craft, a few good opportunities, and a bit of luck, you can one day see your name on the silver screen beneath the words "Written By." And when you do, you'll know it was all worthwhile.